KU-469-435

3 JELLIPLAYS

ANN JELLICOE

FABER & FABER
3 Queen Square London

First published in 1975
by Faber and Faber Limited
3 Queen Square London WC1
Printed in Great Britain by
Whitstable Litho, Straker Brothers Ltd

All rights reserved

ISBN 0 571 10705 2

All rights whatsoever in these plays are strictly
reserved and applications for permission to perform
them, etc. must be made in advance, before
rehearsals begin, to Margaret Ramsay Ltd., 14a
Goodwin's Court, St. Martin's Lane, London W.C.2.

CONDITIONS OF SALE
This book is sold subject to the condition that it shall
not, by way of trade or otherwise, be lent, re-sold,
hired out or otherwise circulated without the pub-
lisher's prior consent in any form of binding or
cover other than that in which it is published and
without a similar condition including this condition
being imposed on the subsequent purchaser

© 1975 by Ann Jellicoe

3 JELLIPLAYS

QUEEN MARGARET COLLEGE LIBRAR*

other plays by Ann Jellicoe

for adults

THE SPORT OF MY MAD MOTHER
THE KNACK
SHELLEY or THE IDEALIST
THE GIVEAWAY

FOR TOM

CONTENTS

<u>Clever Elsie, Smiling John, Silent Peter</u> and <u>A Good
Thing or a Bad Thing</u> were produced in a double bill
by the Royal Court Young People's Theatre Scheme
at the Theatre Upstairs, Royal Court Theatre,
London S. W. 1, on January 29th 1974, with the
following cast:

CLEVER ELSIE, SMILING JOHN, SILENT PETER

Clever Elsie	Janet Legge
Mother	Judy Buxton
Father	Colin Bennett
Smiling John	Stephen McKenna
Silent Peter	Tony Robertson

A GOOD THING OR A BAD THING

Jack	Stephen McKenna
Mother	Colin Bennett
Monster	Tony Robertson
Princess	Janet Legge
Queen	Judy Buxton

Directed by Ann Jellicoe
Designed by David Short
Lighting by John Tindale

YOU'LL NEVER GUESS!

YOU'LL NEVER GUESS! First produced by the
Unicorn Theatre for Young People at the Arts
Theatre, Great Newport St., London W.C.2 on
May 19th 1973, with the following cast:

Dwarf	Richard Jaques
Baltasar	Ian Ruskin
Anna	Jaqueline Andrews
Miller	Sion Probert
King	Eric Leroy
Grand Duke of Tuscany	Gary Fairhall
Miss Thistlewaite	Marina McConnell
Pikeman 1	Peter Kosta
Pikeman 2	Lewis Barber

Directed by Ann Jellicoe
Designed by Fay Barrett
Lighting by Chris Pullen
Puppet Adviser: Susan Forster

<u>CAST</u>

DWARF

BALTASAR, the King's adviser

ANNA, the miller's daughter

MILLER

KING

GRAND DUKE OF TUSCANY

MISS THISTLEWAITE

2 PIKEMEN / COURTIERS

WAITING WOMAN

The Dwarf was played by a puppet in the first production. There may well be other solutions as to how
to cast this character but the puppet was interesting,
successful and engaging. It was about 90 cm high,
the body formed of polystyrene and the head of papier
mache, joints were of rope. The puppet was worked
by a puppeteer who was dressed in black nylon velvet
from head to foot, except for his face, which was
covered with black gauze. Two cords on either side
of the puppet's head were attached to a ring encirc-
ling the puppeteer's head; thus whenever the puppeteer
turned or inclined his head the puppet did likewise.
The puppet's arms and hands were controlled by
sticks, about 30 cm long, which were extensions of
the puppet's forearms. His feet were built into a pair
of slippers which were worn by the puppeteer. A cord,
running from the middle of the puppet's back, was
attached to a belt around the puppeteer's waist - this
was merely to help distribute the weight, which would

otherwise have hung entirely from the puppeteer's head. The puppeteer adopted a slightly stooping posture so that his head was approximately 50 cm above the puppet's. While working the puppet, which was essentially an extension of his own body, the puppeteer was so accepted as to be invisible.

Blackout.

Spotlight Stage C. In the spotlight stands the DWARF.
Looks around to make sure he is quite alone. Picks
up stone, digs beneath it. Looks round cautiously
again, and whispers into hole.

DWARF: I've got another secret for you! I have a
new name. Every thousand years I change my
name, I used to be called Rumpelstiltschen . . .
now I'm called . . . oh no! It's too good a secret!
(DWARF dances round spot singing to tune of
"Ach du Lieber Augustin".)

DWARF: I'm such a clever one, clever one, clever one,
I'm such a clever one. Can't catch me!
(Repeat)
(At end of repeat, big flash. Enter BALTASAR.
Lighting change.)

DWARF (Returning FURIOUS): Who made that flash?
Who did that? (To BALTASAR) Did you make
that flash?

BALTASAR: No.

DWARF (To children): Did any of you make that
flash . . . Someone's been monkeying around

with my magic.

(Exit DWARF grumbling.)

BALTASAR: Hello . . . I'm Baltasar, I give the
King advice, and help him. This is a play about
a Dwarf who was clever, but not as clever as
he thought he was; a stupid, lazy miller who
told a thumping lie to save his own skin and made
life very difficult for someone else; a proud and
greedy King; and Anna, the miller's daughter,
who made an unwise promise and tried to wriggle
out of it.

(Rhythmical noise of wheel thumping.)
There's the sound of the mill wheel turning, can
you hear it? Thump, thump, thump. That means
the miller's at work grinding his corn . . . He's
grinding his corn to make flour - you have to
grind a lot of corn to make a sackful.

(During preceding, enter ANNA with spinning-
wheel. She starts to spin.)
And here's Anna, the miller's daughter. Hello.

ANNA: Hello.

BALTASAR: What are you doing?

ANNA (ad lib within framework): D'you know what
this is? That's right! It's a spinning-wheel.
(Exit BALTASAR.) Look - there's a foot pedal
here and when I work it with my foot it turns the
wheel . . . The wheel turning makes the spindle
go round. . . . That's the spindle in there, it's
a long piece of metal . . . when the spindle turns

18

the wool is twisted so that it forms a thread,
and then the thread winds on to the bobbin here -
that's the bobbin round the spindle. So you see
this great big wheel doesn't actually make the
thread itself, it's just a device to turn the spindle,
it's the spindle that spins the thread.

D'you know what this is? . . . It's wool just as
it comes off the sheep's back - you sometimes
see it caught in the hedges in the country, don't
you? You can't make clothes of it when it's like
this, you have to make it into thread. First
you must tease the wool so that all the strands
are more or less separate - we call it <u>carding</u> -
these are the carders, pieces of wood with lots
of bits of wire sticking up. You lay bits of the
raw wool on the carders like this and then you
draw them across each other so . . .

You don't see many real spinning-wheels now,
do you? We mostly use machines. But in the old
days everything was spun by hand. What sort of
materials do you spin, d'you know . . . wool?
Cotton? Flax? Silk? . . .

D'you see? It's getting softer and more combed
out, all the strands are being separated and
beginning to lie the same way. Now you take the
wool off the carders like this and roll it a bit . . .
and you have what's called a <u>Rolag</u>. That's a
funny name, isn't it? Rolag.
Now you add the end of the rolag into the bit of

wool that's already on the bobbin. Now we're ready to spin. I set the wheel going and I draw the rolag out and the strands are twisted . . . and the thread winds on to the bobbin . . . twist and . . . wind. Twist and . . . wind. Twist and wind . . . . And that's spinning.

(Sound of the mill-wheel thumping comes to a stop.)

Listen! Hasn't the mill wheel stopped turning? My father must have knocked off. Stopping work already! And we've no money. Look! This is where I keep the housekeeping - it's empty - nothing there. I do wish he'd work a bit harder. It would be wonderful to have some new clothes. Here I spin all day long and everything I spin has to be sold so that we can buy food to eat.

(Enter MILLER, carrying small sack of flour half full. Doesn't see ANNA. Goes to house-keeping box and finds it empty.)

ANNA: Is that all you've done?

MILLER: Don't be cheeky.

ANNA: Why aren't you working at the mill?

MILLER: Got a pain.

ANNA: You give me a pain. Stopping work after you've only ground half a sack.

MILLER: Been milling since three o'clock this morning.

ANNA: Three o'clock! You were still lying in bed at ten. Wheel's only been turning half an hour, hasn't it, children?

MILLER: Don't talk to your father like that. Sacks
and sacks back there.

ANNA: Sacks and sacks _full_?

MILLER: I'm tired, I've had enough for today. I'm
going to see the King.

ANNA: There's work to be - what!

MILLER: Have you got any money?

ANNA: You're going to see the King!

MILLER: I can look, can't I? Have you got any money?

ANNA: I need money to buy food. You give me some
money.

MILLER: I haven't got any.

ANNA: Let's see your pockets.

MILLER: I haven't got any.

ANNA: Five p!. . . And another five p!

MILLER: How can I go and see the King with nothing
to jingle?

ANNA: How can we eat?

MILLER: Oh, well. Looking's free, I suppose.

(Exit MILLER and ANNA in different directions.

Enter DWARF. Wheel struck. Throne, etc. on.)

DWARF (ad lib): He was a jolly fellow, wasn't he?
Why not go off in the middle of the day if you feel
like it? Bit hard on his daughter, though . . .

Would you like to go and visit a King? What
are Kings like, d'you think?

(Fanfare. Enter PIKEMEN.)

SERVANT (off distant): Make way for His Majesty the

21

King!

SERVANT (off nearer): Make way for His Majesty
the King!

SERVANT (off near): Make way for His Majesty the
King!

(Music. SERVANTS enter backwards bowing.
Enter BALTASAR. Enter KING. The KING is a
bit small and wizened, like James I. He has a
particular mannerism, which he unconsciously
uses whenever his mind is running on a scheme
to make money.)

BALTASAR: His Majesty is prepared to give audience.
Draw near without trembling and make your
requests and problems known to the King, the
father of his people. Come now, anybody want to
ask the King anything?

DWARF: I wouldn't if I were you. He's so greedy,
any favours he gives he always wants to be paid
for them.

BALTASAR: His Grace the Grand Duke of Tuscany
craves audience with His Majesty.

KING: The Grand Duke of Tuscany?

BALTASAR: Owns all the lands south of your kingdom,
Sire. Almost as rich as you yourself.

KING: Indeed? (pause) Let the Grand Duke approach.

SERVANT (off distant): His Grace the Grand Duke of
Tuscany. Let him approach.

DWARF: Here's the Grand Duke.

SERVANT (off nearer): His Grace the Grand Duke of

22

Tuscany. Let him approach!

DWARF: People are always insulting him and he has to go and fight them.

SERVANT (off near): His Grace the Grand Duke of Tuscany. Let him approach!

DWARF: Strong people never insult him, so he never has to fight them.

(Enter GRAND DUKE, a magnificent-looking soldier of fortune in great boots and a plumed hat, but he is really the cowardly braggart captain of the Commedia dell'Arte. The GRAND DUKE makes an elaborate entrance but a PIKE-MAN, bowing behind, jabs his bottom with his pike. GRAND DUKE rounds on him and belabours him with a feather.)

GRAND DUKE: I have been grossly - Grossly - Grossly insulted by the kingdom of Luxemia.

KING: Grossly insulted?

GRAND DUKE: One of their cows -

KING: Cows?

GRAND DUKE: Stepped -

KING: Stepped?

GRAND DUKE: One of their cows stepped on my second gardener's - Oh, no, it's too much!

KING: My dear fellow!

GRAND DUKE: One of their cows stepped on my second gardener's -

KING: Yes?

GRAND DUKE: Big toe.

KING: What!

GRAND DUKE: A gross insult! A very gross insult!
Grossly insulted! Aagh! Gross! Gross! Gross!

KING: Please!

GRAND DUKE: Gross! Gross! Grocers! Grocers!
Half a pound of sugar and a quarter of tea.

KING: Am I to understand that you wish to avenge
this insult from Luxemia?

GRAND DUKE: Hah! Let me have at them! Don't
try to restrain me! Don't hold me back! Hah!
Hah!
(GRAND DUKE fences with imaginary assailant.)

DWARF: Now why should a peaceful little country
like Luxemia insult the Grand Duke? They're
only interested in their cows.

GRAND DUKE (continuing): Give me my spears and
muskets! Bring me my cannon! Glory on the
barricades! Death! Death! Strike! Strike!
March! March! Form fours! Present arms!
(The GRAND DUKE has momentarily lost his way
again. From having been in the battlefield he has
brought himself to the parade ground. On the
order the PIKEMAN beside him comes to attention
with a crash and brings his pike down on the
GRAND DUKE's foot. The GRAND DUKE howls
in agony and sits down to nurse his injury.)

KING: Now. In order to avenge this "insult" he, and
his army, must cross my kingdom. He needs to
cross my kingdom in order to reach Luxemia.

24

(To BALTASAR) Luxemia - peaceful little
country.

BALTASAR: Very rich, Sire, annual income four
million crowns.

KING: Four million crowns, eh? (pause) You may
march.

GRAND DUKE: Your Majesty! Sire! I thank you!
Gracious . . . noble . . . magnanimous . . .

KING: But -

GRAND DUKE: Yes?

KING: Having - avenged - the insult in Luxemia you
will naturally seize - find yourself the unwilling
possessor - of a fair amount of loot - gold and
jewels. I understand Luxemia is a reasonably
prosperous little country. In return for favours
received you must pay me three million crowns.

GRAND DUKE: Three million crowns?

KING: Three million.

GRAND DUKE: But the annual income is only worth
four million crowns.

KING (petulantly, to BALTASAR): You said six
million.

BALTASAR: Well, er, actually -

KING: He says six million.

GRAND DUKE: Four million.

KING: Very well, I agree, four million.

GRAND DUKE: No, but that's the -

KING: My dear fellow, don't haggle. If the annual
income alone is four million, think what the

25

Gross National Product must be! Four million
or you don't cross.

GRAND DUKE: But that only leaves me -

KING: Take it or leave it.

(Pause.)

GRAND DUKE (swallowing): I take it.

KING: Well done, my dear fellow! I congratulate you!
Dear me, you do drive a hard bargain, I shall
have to watch you or you'll have the boots off
my feet! Hah ha! Off you go now and avenge your
insult. Good hunting.

(Exit GRAND DUKE. Cod trip. Exit PIKEMAN
(he returns with Miss Thistlewaite's luggage).
Enter MILLER unobserved.)

MILLER (ad lib): Here I am. I got in while everyone
was watching that big fellow.

Look at all that gold, whew! And the mirrors!
And all those fine clothes, the lace and the braid
and - if only Anna could see them she'd never
be content with spinning again.

SERVANT (far): Miss Alice Matilda Thistlewaite.

KING: Who is this Miss Thistlewaite?

SERVANT (nearer): Miss Alice Matilda Thistlewaite.

BALTASAR: You sent for her, Sire.

SERVANT (near): Miss Alice Matilda Thistlewaite.

(Enter ALICE MATILDA THISTLEWAITE, a
Victorian lady of no nonsense. She is sensibly
dressed for crossing Africa in a costume not
unlike that she would wear for visiting Norfolk.

She carries an umbrella over her arm. She has a large amount of luggage. She observes the KING through a glass.)

MISS T. : Rex Imperious. A not uncommon species.

BALTASAR: Eminent botanist, about to cross the continent of Africa in search of rare plants.

A COURTIER: Alone?

(Titters from the other COURTIERS.)

MISS T. : Naturally alone. I am an unmarried lady. (More titters. MISS T. regards the COURTIERS through her glass and quells them.) Noblessus vulgaris - the common courtier - and a poor specimen.

KING: Miss Thistlewaite! I am delighted that you have come to see me on the eve of your momentous journey. I sent for you because - because I wanted to make the acquaintance of a lady of such intrepid - such dauntless . . .

MISS T. : Your Majesty is very kind but I have already encountered the equatorial jungles of South America -

BALTASAR (aside to KING): Notable collection of orchids!

KING: Your orchids are world famous.

MISS T. (gratified): Your Majesty is very well informed. (KING makes a modest gesture.) But I assure you crossing Africa is no more dangerous than crossing the Highlands - provided that, mentally and physically, one is properly equipped for every

27

eventuality.

KING: Every - ?

MISS T. : From running out of cocoa to cannibalism.

KING: And what would be your attitude to such disasters, Miss Thistlewaite?

MISS T. : To endure the unpleasant as long as I may and accept the inevitable when I must.

KING: Even cannibalism?

MISS T. : I trust I may be killed before I am eaten.

KING: You seem to have everything you need.

MISS T. : Very little is procurable south of Cairo. I do not believe in inviting disaster through sloppy preparation. I take with me everthing that good sense may suggest and the Army and Navy Stores provide.

KING: A canvas washstand, very ingenious. Beads?

MISS T. : For barter.

KING: And this?

MISS T:: My portable medicine chest. Quinine, brandy (for medicinal purposes), sal volatile, aspirin powders. Oil of cloves for toothache.

KING: Toothache?

MISS T. : Toothache is the only thing I really fear in the jungle.

KING: I am lost in admiration of your foresight and method. (MISS T. visibly flattered.)
(KING signals to PIKEMAN who exits.)
Will you allow me to present you with a small, an insignificant, gift?

MISS T. : Your Majesty is very kind but -

KING: I know you have thought of everything, but I
flatter myself that you haven't got one of these.
(Claps his hands. Enter PIKEMAN with piece of
equipment.)
This, Miss Thistlewaite, is a small apparatus
for testing samples of soil.

MISS T. : Testing soil?

KING: You place a little soil here, and add a few
drops of this liquid, and this . . . and if the
paper turns pink, then I want you to make a note
of the precise place, the precise spot, where
you found that soil - and let me know.

MISS T. : I see.

KING: That should not be beyond the powers of a
botanist - even a lady botanist.
(Gentle applause from COURTIERS.)

MISS T. : Soil here . . . add this (she looks at liquid,
smells it, tastes it). If the paper turns pink . . .
I see. Thank you but no.

KING (amazed): You return . . . !

MISS T. : This is Porsche's test for the presence of
gold in soil and rock, is it not?

KING (to BALTASAR, pretending innocence): Is it?

MISS T. : With this apparatus one may test for the
presence of gold in soil. You wish me, in crossing
Africa on my botanical expedition, to keep a
precise record of any place where gold may be
found.

29

KING: That's it precisely . . . I knew . . .

MISS T. : I go to Africa to increase the boundaries
of knowledge, not to expose the ignorant savage
to the grossest forms of commercial exploitation.
Good day, sir.

(KING flabbergasted, MISS T. is going.)

KING: Arrest that woman!

(PIKEMAN makes for MISS T. who raises her
umbrella. PIKEMAN grabs the end of the umbrella,
which comes away in his hand, as with a sword
stick. The handle remains with MISS T. with an
exotic-looking orchid attached to it.)

MISS T. : I would advise you not to lay hands on me,
young man.

KING: Arrest her! Well, get on with it.

MISS T. : Not a step closer.

KING: What have you got there?

MISS T. : A rare species of orchid, Astrogalus
Digitalis Rex. It has coarse hairs, rather like
Urtica dioica, or the common stinging nettle,
but unlike a nettle the sting of this is quite lethal.
Anyone touching it will die in five minutes, and
a very unpleasant death that will be.

(Pause.)

KING (through clenched teeth): You may go, Miss
Thistlewaite.

MISS T. : Good day, sir.

(Exit MISS T. KING furious.)

DWARF: Golly! She frightened me - did she frighten

30

you? Now I come to think of it, she's the sort
of person I'd like to have on a desert island -
she'd know which plants you could eat, and what
to do if you broke your leg. I wonder what she'd
be like to have as an aunt? What'd she be like
at home?

(MILLER imitates a fanfare off.)

MILLER (as if distant): Matthew the Miller, let him
approach!

(nearer) Matthew the Miller, let him approach!
(as near) Matthew the Miller, let him approach!
(Enter MILLER.)

KING: Who is this fellow? He doesn't look very clean.
Does he smell?

Never mind. It looks good if I occasionally
receive one of the common people.

MILLER: Matthew the Miller.

BALTASAR: Your Majesty.

MILLER: Oh, I know it's his majesty.

KING: You have come to beg a favour? Approach
without fear - you see? I really do have the
common touch.

MILLER: Well yes, or, no not really your majesty.
I was just looking.

KING: Just looking?

MILLER: I just thought I'd like to look - to gaze.

KING: Fine, go ahead, no obligation . . . D'you
think I could charge people for looking?

BALTASAR: Make them pay?

31

KING: Like the waxworks. Might be quite . . . That
  will be 5p.

MILLER: Eh?

KING: 5p.

MILLER: For looking?

KING: 5p for looking.

MILLER: I haven't got 5p.

KING: I'm not asking three million crowns, you know.
  You come here gazing, wasting my time. Gazing!
  Looking! Well, what have you got?

MILLER: I - er . . .

  (PIKEMAN threatens.)

MILLER: I -

KING: Have you got power?

MILLER: No, I -

  (PIKEMAN threatens.)

KING: Brains?

  (PIKEMAN threatens.)

MILLER: No, I've - I've got -

KING: Yes?

MILLER: A daughter -

  (Roar of derision. PIKEMAN threatens.)

  Who can spin -

  (PIKEMAN threatens.)

  Straw into gold!

  (Pause.)

MILLER (hardly knowing what he's saying, but
  thinking it must have been something clever as
  he now has everyone's complete attention): I've

32

got a daughter who can spin straw into gold.

(Pause.)

KING: Wool into cloth.

MILLER: That too but -

KING: Flax into linen.

MILLER: Yes, of course, but -

KING: Are you joking?

(PIKEMAN threatens.)

MILLER: No, no.

(KING gestures, PIKEMAN falls back.)

I'm not.

KING: You have a daughter who can spin straw into gold.

MILLER: Straw into gold.

KING: Straw into gold.

(Pause.)

KING: Well, I've got plenty of straw.

(KING mannerism.)

Bring her here.

MILLER: Eh?

KING: I want to see this girl who can spin straw into gold.

(Ordered pandemonium. Voices ring across each other, actors cross and recross stage removing throne, carpet, etc. Bring on spinning wheel.)

VOICES: The King commands the Miller's daughter who can spin straw into gold. (Repeat from various directions and distances.)

(DWARF dances around stage during change,

echoing the lines: "The King commands! The King commands!" etc. Enter ANNA. Fanfare. Enter KING. KING signals. Enter SERVANT with straw. Exit SERVANT.)

KING: Spin this into gold by the first cockcrow or by the second cockcrow you will die the death.

ANNA: Die.

KING: The death.

(Clock begins to strike midnight. Exit KING.)

ANNA (to children): Do you know how to spin straw into gold? Help me! Help me! Do you know? Do you? I can't spin straw, I told you it's too brittle, look, it's not like wool, it breaks, it won't spin. I can't spin it, much less spin it into -

(Last stroke of clock. ANNA sinks down. Pause.)

DWARF: You need me. I can do it. Go on, tell her I can help her. I can. I can do anything.

ANNA: What? What? Who? Can you?

DWARF: Simple! Child's play! (laughing contemptuously) Spin straw into gold!

ANNA: But how? How?

DWARF: Magic -

ANNA: Magic?

DWARF: Yes, magic.

ANNA: But how?

DWARF (irritated): Oh, don't go on. Can't tell you. Can't explain.

ANNA: But -

DWARF: If you're going to go on like this, I can't be

34

bothered.

ANNA: Oh please! I do need you. Will you spin it for
me?

DWARF: What'll you give me?

ANNA: To -

DWARF: A bargain's a bargain.

ANNA: Spin -

DWARF: One good turn deserves -

ANNA: I've got 5p.

DWARF: Let's see - done.

DWARF: I'm such a clever one! Such a clever one!
Such a clever one!

I'm such a clever one! Can't catch me!

(Repeat.)

(At the end of repeat the DWARF starts to spin.
(Wheel has a piece of gold tinsel attached to the
bobbin.) Immediately cross fade lights: blackout
onstage, some lights in auditorium. Exit DWARF.
Enter GRAND DUKE at back of auditorium blowing
a trumpet.)

GRAND DUKE: Out! Out of my way! Forward the
Tuscan armies! Revenge! Ha! The enemy! Form!
Form! Close the ranks! Charge! (Cows moo.)
I am the Grand Duke of Tuscany. (Moo) There!
There! Here! Here! Have at you! (Moo moo)
Hand it over! Let me through! (Moo) Take me
to your leader! Agh! Agh! (Moo) Don't do that!
I say I am the Grand Duke of Tuscany. (Mmmooo)
Stop it! Stop it! (Moo) No, don't, please, I'm

35

ticklish, no stop it! Do, do stop! Don't do that!
(Moo) (Cow moos take over protests and pleas.
Fade light.)
(During this diversion in the auditorium the bale
of straw is covered with a net of gold (steel wool
sprayed gold, with tinsels, sequins and, above
all, curled gold foil will answer). Exit GRAND
DUKE. Cross fade to stage lights. ANNA asleep.
Cockcrow. Fanfare. Enter KING and BALTASAR
with scales.)

KING: Assay it.

BALTASAR: True gold, Sire, the finest.

KING: 22 carat?

BALTASAR: The finest.

(Pause. KING signals, SERVANTS remove gold
and bring in larger bale of straw. Exit all but
KING.)

KING: Spin this straw into gold by the first cockcrow
or by the second cockcrow you will die the death.
(Exit KING.)

DWARF: Well?

ANNA: 5p. It's my last.

DWARF: Done.

I'm such a clever one! Such a clever one!
Such a clever one!
I'm such a clever one! Can't catch me!
(Repeat.)
(DWARF starts to spin as before. Exit DWARF.
Enter MEN with banners of light-weight silk

about 5 or six metres long. They weave this into
fantastic patterns. Meanwhile the straw is changed
upstage. Exit BANNERS. Cockcrow. Fanfare.
Enter KING L.)

KING: 24 carat?

BALTASAR: The finest.

(Pause. KING signals, SERVANTS enter with
larger bale.)

ANNA: I won't.

KING: What?

ANNA: I won't spin any more.

KING: Then you shall -

ANNA: Kill me, I don't care. Every day you'll bring
larger and larger bales of straw. I'd rather die . . .
If he puts me to death I won't be able to spin
any more, will I? So he won't have his gold. So
what's the point of killing me? Go on, put me to
death. Then you won't have your gold.
(Pause.)

KING: I see you are a girl of spirit. I'll give you a
choice. If you do not spin this straw into gold by
first cockcrow then by the second cockcrow you
will die the death. But if you do spin and make
all this into gold, then I shall make you my
Queen.

ANNA: Queen!

KING: You shall be Queen. I would not want a girl of
your talents to fall to anyone else. And so I say:
none other shall have you: if you do not spin the

37

straw you shall die. If you do spin it you shall
be my Queen.

(Exit KING.)

ANNA: What can I give you?

DWARF: You find it, I'll do it.

ANNA: No money, no jewels.

DWARF: A bargain's a bargain.

ANNA: When I'm Queen you can have anything, I'll
give you anything.

DWARF: Don't want money.

ANNA: I'll give you anything.

DWARF: Don't want jewels.

ANNA: I'll give you a -

DWARF: Just want -

ANNA: Well?

DWARF: Something living!

ANNA: Something living!

DWARF: Give me your firstborn.

ANNA: My -

DWARF: Your first baby.

ANNA: I couldn't give you my -

DWARF: It's nothing, you won't notice. I want a
friend, someone small like me to play with. If
you don't give him to me I shan't spin that straw
and then you'll be dead anyway. You won't be
Queen and you won't have any children or anything.
So there.

(Pause.)

ANNA: Well -

DWARF: You will!

ANNA: I'll -

DWARF: I'll do it. I'll do it.

    (Sings with great satisfaction:)

        Oh! I'm such a clever one! Such a clever one!
        Such a clever one!

        Oh! I'm such a clever one! Can't catch me!

    (Repeat.)

    (DWARF starts to spin. Cross fade light on
    DWARF upstage to ANNA downstage.)

ANNA: After all, what does it matter? (Pause.)
Maybe he'll forget. (Pause.) Maybe he won't
want it. (Pause.) Maybe I won't have any children
anyway.

    (Blackout at end of ANNA's speech. Wheel etc.
    struck. Exit ANNA and DWARF. Enter BALTASAR.)

BALTASAR (try and get a real discussion going with
children): Would you like to be Queen? Would you
have made that promise to the Dwarf? D'you
think she was right to make that promise? Do
you think the Dwarf will remember the promise?
Do you think it's a good idea to promise things
ahead? If you knew you were going to get a big
bar of chocolate next week, would you promise it
in return for an ice cream now? Would you promise
to give your next year's Christmas present in
return for something you wanted now? What if you
didn't know but you were going to get a bike or a
puppy for Christmas, what would you do when you

found you were going to get a bike? . . . (etc.
etc. ad lib. When ANNA has made change to
Queen:)

Do you think Anna kept her promise? . . . I'll
tell you. Well, the straw was spun into gold, and
the miller's daughter became Queen and did no
more spinning . . .

(Enter QUEEN followed by PIKEMAN. Enter
COURTIER, bows to her.)

And there passed a year and a day, and the
Queen bore a daughter, a little girl who was the
pride of her life and the joy of her heart . . .

(Enter WAITING WOMAN, presents QUEEN
with baby. EXEUNT L.)

At first the Queen remembered the dwarf and
her promise and was fearful for her little daughter,
but as time passed and nothing happened the
memory grew dim, as memories will, and she
was less afraid, until in a little while she almost
forgot her promise to the dwarf altogether . . .

(Laughter off. Enter QUEEN blindfolded,
WAITING WOMAN and COURTIER, they chase
upstage and exit.)

But the dwarf had not forgotten. He waited for
the Queen to send him her baby as she had
promised, and when the baby didn't come the
dwarf determined to get her himself . . .

(Enter DWARF. Re-enter QUEEN, WAITING
WOMAN and PIKEMAN still playing blind man's

buff. As they play, the DWARF slips amongst them and magics WAITING WOMAN, COURTIER and BALTASAR in turn. As he gestures (music off), they freeze.)

QUEEN: Baltasar! Baltasar!

(QUEEN, horrified, sees the effect of the magic, then sees DWARF.)

No!

DWARF: You seem to have been avoiding me.

QUEEN: No, no.

DWARF: A bargain's a bargain. If it wasn't for me you wouldn't be Queen now.

QUEEN: Take my jewels, take anything you want but leave me my baby.

DWARF: Don't want gold, don't want jewels, want a baby to play with, I'm lonely. Go on, children. Tell her to give me the baby.

QUEEN: Oh, children, please, what shall I do? I'll give you anything.

DWARF: Don't want crown, don't want robes, want baby.

(QUEEN weeps.)

Oh, you are silly. You make a bargain and then you don't want to keep it. Oh stop it, stop it, shut up. Can't stand crying. Oh, you. Tell you what, since you want to keep the silly little thing so much, I'll ask you a riddle -

QUEEN: A riddle?

DWARF: And I'll give you three days to answer, and

I'll come three times. And if you can tell me the
answer to the riddle you can keep your baby.

QUEEN: Oh, children, you'll help me, won't you?
Baltasar! (BALTASAR and OTHERS still frozen.
DWARF magics them back to life.)
What's the riddle?

DWARF: Are you ready?

QUEEN: Yes we are, aren't we?

DWARF: What's -

QUEEN: Yes?

DWARF: What's my name?

QUEEN: What's your name?

DWARF (hugging himself with glee): What's my name?

QUEEN: I'm sure we can find the answer to that, can't
we, children. Can we have as many guesses as
we like? Now what names can we think of?

BALTASAR: Is your name Rumpelstiltschen?

DWARF: No, it's not.

ALL: It's not Rumpelstiltschen.
(ALL encourage children to call out names.
DWARF can hardly contain himself. When noise
gets too thunderous, fade to blackout. Exeunt
all but DWARF. Light up. Enter QUEEN, WAIT -
ING WOMAN, COURTIER, BALTASAR.)

QUEEN: A day has passed, I have travelled as far as
I may and my servants have crossed the land and
we have many, many names, some of them very
strange.

QUEEN: Is your name Shortibs?

42

DWARF: No.

QUEEN: Leanshanks?

DWARF: No, no. You'll never guess. Save yourself the trouble. You may as well give me the baby now.

QUEEN: More names, children.

(QUEEN, PIKEMAN and BALTASAR take names from audience and repeat them. QUEEN gets more despondent, DWARF more cocky. Noise gets louder. Exeunt all but DWARF. Fade to blackout. Spot centre. In spot DWARF. Behaves as if he is in a secret place. Looking around him, giggling, lifts up a stone.)

DWARF: Tee hee! Tee hee hee! Never guess, not in a thousand thousand thousand . . . Ooh! I can't bear it, can't bear it. Such fun. Can't bear it. Must tell someone. (Looks round to make sure noone's about. Whispering into hole.) My name is . . . my name is . . . Bylobog . . . Bylobog . . . (Dances round spotlight, singing.)

    I'm such a clever one! Such a clever one!
    Such a clever one!
    I'm such a clever one -
    My name is Bylobog!

(Lights fade to blackout. Lights up. Enter QUEEN, WAITING WOMAN, PIKEMAN, BALT-ASAR. All very tired and depressed.)

QUEEN (if she gets a chance): I've searched everywhere. I've no names, have you any idea what his name

43

can be?

(Enter DWARF.)

ALL: Your name is Bylobog!

(DWARF furious; he stumps about swearing and raging. Finally he stamps his foot so hard he gets it stuck in the ground.)

QUEEN: Ssh! His foot's stuck - can't you get it free?

DWARF (reluctant): Have to do some magic.

QUEEN: What?

DWARF: Have to do some magic . . . Well . . .
Don't look at me - Don't listen! . . . You mustn't see my magic. Mustn't! Turn away - go on! Close your eyes!

(They turn away. Pause.)

Abracadabra! Abracadabra! (To his intense chagrin his leg won't come free. Getting more and more excited and despairing:) Casaweyla! Modignates! Modignates! (Finally in desperation he whispers his most secret word:) Koobomem! (louder) Koobomem! (desperate shouting) Koobomem! (He collapses crying.)

QUEEN: Bylobog, you're so clever and know so much magic. Why can't you get your foot free?

DWARF: It must be because you know my name.

QUEEN: What?

DWARF: Now you know my name, my magic, it's all gone.

QUEEN: Oh Bylobog.

DWARF: I do wish you'd stop shouting my name all

44

over the place and help get me free.

QUEEN: Try pulling.

(ALL line up and try and pull DWARF free.)

DWARF: 1 . . . 2 . . . 3 . . . Heave! Heave! . . .
No good.

QUEEN: Try again.

DWARF: Well, be careful, it's almost pulling me in
half. All my stuffing will fall out. Ready?

ALL: Yes.

DWARF: 1 . . . 2 . . . 3 . . . Heave! Heave! Heave!
(ALL fall over in heap.)

QUEEN: Perhaps if you think of a new name and don't
tell us your magic will come back.

DWARF (impatient): Oh yes, yes, it will but that takes
ages . . . I can see I'm just going to have to teach
you all some magic.

QUEEN: Magic, me?

DWARF: All of you, all the children, everyone.

QUEEN: But I haven't any magic.

DWARF: Everyone's got some magic, but it's so weak
and little, they don't know they've got it. Now if
you all work your magic together it's just possible
it might be strong enough to get my foot free.
Right now, first you've all got to learn the magic
words Yasram Otaga - say it with me - Yasram
Otaga . . . Yasram Otaga. Now you mustn't
shout it, that's no good, you'll just spread your
magic around whereas we want it here . Now make
a funnel of your hands.

45

QUEEN: Like this?

DWARF: That's right, and point the funnel towards my
foot and whisper Yasram Otaga. Ready? Right.

ALL: Yasram Otaga.

DWARF: I think it's easier . . . I think it's a bit
easier . . . You'll have to try harder than this,
you know. Now let's have it again. Yasram Otaga -
just a bit louder this time. Try closing your eyes
and really concentrating. Go on, close your eyes
now when I say three: 1 . . . 2. . . 3. . .

ALL: Yasram Otaga.

DWARF: Yes! It's better, it's better. Once more, and
really try! This time give it all you've got, as
loud as you can! 1 . . . 2 . . . 3 . . .

ALL: Yasram Otaga!

DWARF: I'm free, I'm free! Oh I'm so clever! You're
so clever! I'm so clever to teach you to be clever.
Well, I'm off.

QUEEN: Wait a minute. I feel I owe you something.

DWARF: No, you don't owe me anything. A bargain's
a bargain. You guessed the riddle. You can keep
your baby.

QUEEN: The children guessed the riddle.

DWARF: However did they do it?

QUEEN: Have you got a new name yet?

DWARF: Oh yes, I've got a new name . . . You'll
never guess.

QUEEN: One of the nice things about being a Queen is
that sometimes you can make things happen.

DWARF: Like my magic?

QUEEN: Yes, like your magic. And so I say: I think
you're a rather kind dwarf, you're not as clever
as you think you are, but then none of us are,
come to that. So long as I am Queen there will
always be a welcome for you here at the palace
whenever you would like to come and play with
the baby. . . . What is your favourite food?

DWARF: My favourite food?

QUEEN: Yes. What do you like best to eat?

DWARF: Honey and nuts and raspberry yoghurt.

QUEEN: What do you say, children? Shall we give
him some honey and nuts and raspberry yoghurt?
Shall we? Shall we?

ALL: Shall we give the dwarf honey and nuts and
raspberry yoghurt? (etc. etc. ad lib.)

DWARF (ad lib in character): Hello children, hello
. . . Aren't you going to say hello? Try again,
Hello? That's better but I can't hear you very
well, try again . . . Hello . . . Ah, that's better,
that's better. I like riddles, do you like riddles?
Bet you don't know the answer to my riddles, I'm
so clever: What wobbles as it flies? Do you know
what wobbles as it flies? A Jellycopter! You
didn't know! You didn't know! Oh, I'm so clever!
Oh, I'm so clever! Why did the duck fly south? . . .
Go on, why did the duck fly south? . . . You know?
How did you know? (He is very angry and stamping
his foot.) How did you know? Who told you? Someone told you didn't they? Now I'll ask you a riddle
and you won't know the answer to this one, noone
knows the answer to this one. What's my name?
Go on, tell me what's my name? You'll never
guess, noone knows but me . . . No . . . No, not
that any more, I changed it. What's my name?
Abracadabra! (Gesturing magic.) One! Two!
Three! (Big flash L.)

48

CLEVER ELSIE, SMILING JOHN, SILENT PETER

CAST

FATHER
MOTHER
CLEVER ELSIE
SMILING JOHN
SILENT PETER

SETTING: Simple and Breughel-like.

MUSIC may be used from time to time - tin whistle,
hand bells, drum - played by the actors themselves.

Enter CLEVER ELSIE wearing wreath of flowers and ribbons, MOTHER, FATHER playing pipe. They sit. Pause. MOTHER pours beer. Pause. Enter SMILING JOHN. CLEVER ELSIE offers him beer shyly. They sit. Pause. FATHER stops piping and drinks. Pause.

JOHN: A man wants a clever wife (pause). She must be clever.

(Pause.)

FATHER & MOTHER: Clever Elsie.

(They drink. Pause.)

MOTHER: Clever Elsie. Go and draw some beer from the barrel in the cellar.

(ELSIE rises, takes pitcher and leaves room. JOHN watches the sturdy body.)

IN CELLAR

(Music through scene. ELSIE sets pitcher below barrel, turns on tap. Sits. Becomes aware of something above her head which makes her uneasy. Rises, turns off beer tap. Sits. Starts to cry.

51

QUEEN MARGARET COLLEGE LIBRARY

<u>IN ROOM</u>
(The three sit quietly. Pause. MOTHER rises
and goes.)

<u>IN CELLAR</u>
MOTHER: What's up?
(ELSIE indicates above her head. Both look up.)
ELSIE: The axe! Supposing me and Smiling John got
married and we had a child, and we sent the child
down here to draw beer and the axe hanging up
there fell down on the child's head and killed it.
(She weeps.)
MOTHER (working it out): Supposing you and Smiling
John got married . . . and had a child . . . and
sent the child down here to get beer . . . and the
axe . . . fell down and killed it.
(MOTHER starts to weep. Both sit crying, their
aprons stuffed into their mouths, or over their
heads.)

<u>IN ROOM</u>
(Pause. JOHN looks at his empty beaker. FATHER
rises and exits.)

<u>IN CELLAR</u>
(FATHER looks at two weeping women.)
FATHER: What's up?
ELSIE & MOTHER (weeping and incoherent): The
axe . . . the axe.
52

FATHER: My axe?

ELSIE & MOTHER (speaking across each other):
Supposing Clever Elsie marries Smiling John,
and they have a child, and we send the child down
here to draw some beer, and the axe falls on the
child's head and kills it.

FATHER (beginning to sniff as he talks): Supposing
Smiling John and Clever Elsie get married, and
have a child, and we send the child down here to
draw some beer . . . and the axe . . . falls on
its . . . and . . .
(He can't finish for weeping.)

IN ROOM

(Colossal din from the cellar. JOHN appears to
hear something. Pause. Rises and goes to cellar.)

IN CELLAR

(ELSIE, FATHER and MOTHER ad lib story
across each other.)

FATHER (still moaning): Clever Elsie - she thought
of that.

MOTHER (moaning): She thought of that.

FATHER: Clever Elsie did.

MOTHER: It was Clever Elsie.

ELSIE: I thought of that.

FATHER (realising it was very clever): Clever Elsie
thought of that.

MOTHER (ditto): Clever Elsie thought of that.

ELSIE (intense satisfaction): I thought of that.

    (JOHN follows story slowly. Nods in solemn
    satisfaction.)

JOHN: Clever Elsie . . . Clever Elsie . . . She shall
    be my wife.

    (He holds out his hand palm uppermost, she lays
    her hand on his palm to palm. All dance. Exeunt.
    Pause. Re-enter ELSIE and JOHN.)

IN ROOM

    (ELSIE has removed wreath and wears a kerchief.
    She and JOHN eating.)

JOHN: Hay's ready.

    (Pause. ELSIE eats.)

    Hay's ready for cutting.

    (Pause. She eats.)

    So you cut.

    (Pause. She eats.)

    I'm going to market.

    (She stops eating.)

    To sell some sheep.

    (Pause.)

ELSIE: I want to come to market.

JOHN: You cut hay.

    (Exit JOHN. ELSIE rises, gets a kerchief, puts
    bread and cheese in it. Gets a bottle of beer.
    Gets sickle. Goes to field.)

AT MARKET

*(Enter JOHN with sheep (sound of bleating).
Drives sheep into pen and leans watching them.
Remains unmoving and unconcerned during
following. JOHN never smiles. Enter SILENT
PETER, tall and thin; he wears a hat sewn round
with bells which jingle as he talks.*

PETER: Hello! Hello! My good friend John! Well, if
it isn't my good friend John! You remember me?
Silent Peter! Long time no see! Where's Clever
Elsie? She not here today? Prettier than ever, I
guess. Keeping her at home, are you? out of
harm's way? Ha ha! Keeping her to yourself?
Looking after the house, I daresay. Oh. You've
got a good one there. Any little ones yet? Once
they come, they come in dozens. They come in
dozens once they come. These your sheep? You
selling these sheep? Not very good, are they?
Pretty mangy lot they look to me. Funny you
should be wanting to get rid of these sheep.
Wouldn't mind buying a few sheep myself, if they
were reasonable, you know, if the price was
right. What you want for them? Two pounds?
Poor beasts like that. Two pounds, what you
say? Look at those hooves now, all split. Where
you been letting them run? And that fleece! Call
that fleece? There's no wool there. What you been
feeding them on? That grass of yours, that's no
keep, no goodness in it. You can see that from

55

the state of these poor beasts. Say two pounds
fifty? Two pounds fifty! I'm mad to offer it for
animals like these. You can't give away sheep
like that. Three pounds. I'm beggaring myself.
It's charity, that's what. Three pounds, what
you say? Three pounds? It's my final offer.
(ELSIE IN FIELD sits down and opens her food.
She eats during next part of speech and then
falls asleep.)
Three pounds. You're mad to turn it down, think
again. If I don't take these sheep - call 'em
sheep! If I don't take these poor suffering beasts
off your hands they'll pass out on their feet. Four
pounds, that's what I said. Did I hear myself say
four pounds? I must be dreaming! I'll not go no
higher. They got better down the market, you
know. I only got to go down. How many more you
got at home like this? I'd be afraid to let people
see them, I'd be ashamed, I would. I wouldn't
like to expose them to the fresh air, the shock
might kill 'em. What's that then? What's that?
It could be foot rot. Could be. Take a look! Go
on, take a look! Foot rot if my name isn't Silent
Peter.
(JOHN is taking an interest in PETER's hat. He
takes PETER's hat off his head and looks at it.)
I dare say you're in a hurry, all this hanging
around waiting for a . . . Good hat, eh? You
see those bells? You see those bells? My idea,

56

took my fancy, like to jingle. Four pounds fifty.
(JOHN puts PETER's hat on to his own head and
gives PETER his hat.)
Ha ha! Very funny! Four pounds fifty.
(PETER reaches for his hat. JOHN stops him
with a gesture, holding up five fingers.)
Five pounds? Five pounds! You're mad. Five
pounds! I'm not paying five pounds for those
decrepit - Good day!
(PETER starts to exit.)
Good day! (pause) Oh, all right . . . . Five
pounds.
(JOHN turns briskly. They strike hands three
times to seal bargain. PETER counts out notes.)
1 - I don't know why I'm doing this. 2 - it's
daylight robbery. 3 - I'd only do it for a friend.
4 - they'll die before I get 'em back home, I'll
have to carry them. 5 - Now let's have my hat.
What about my hat?
(JOHN exits L. still with PETER's hat on his
head. PETER starts to follow. Enter IMAGINARY
CHARACTER. PETER dashes back to him.)
Good day, sir! Good day! You interested in some
fine sheep? You want to buy some sheep? Fleece
like gold, sir! Here take a look. Ten pounds,
sir? How about ten pounds?

IN FIELD. DAY
(Enter ELSIE cutting hay. Music. After a while

music is superceded by bird noises. ELSIE sits.
Eats bread, throws crumbs to birds. Drinks beer.
Music. ELSIE falls asleep. Music drowsily imit-
ates her.)

NIGHT

(Owl hooting. Enter JOHN with lantern. Goes
into house.)

JOHN (calling): Clever Elsie! Clever Elsie! (annoyed)
House not clean . . . . Tea not ready . . . . Huh.
(comes outside) Clever Elsie!
(Finds her. Pulls off hat angrily. Thinks. Puts
hat on ELSIE's head.)
Let her cool her heels out there for a bit.
(Goes into house. ELSIE stirs, bells jingle. She
wakes.)

ELSIE: Eh? . . . What? . . . Who's there? . . .
What's that? . . . Who's there? . . . Is that you,
Smiling John? . . . (listening, trying to trace
source of jingle) . . . Every time I move . . .
there's a . . . I don't usually . . . I feel funny . . .
I don't feel like me . . . (she shivers, feels her
arm is stiff) . . . Can I be me? (pause) Perhaps
I'm not me . . . (thinks) . . . I know, I'll go home
to Smiling John . . . and I'll ask if I'm there and
if I'm not there I must be here.

AT HOUSE

(ELSIE knocks.)

58

ELSIE: Is that you, Smiling John? You there, Smiling John?

JOHN: Yes, I'm here.

ELSIE: Is Clever Elsie there?

JOHN: Yes, Clever Elsie's there.

(Pause.)

ELSIE: Is she really there?

JOHN: Clever Elsie's there.

ELSIE: Clever Elsie is there with Smiling John. (pause) Then who am I? . . . Who am I? . . . I wish I knew who I was.

(She sits perturbed. Enter SILENT PETER with lantern.)

PETER: I sold those sheep for six pounds and now I've come for my hat. I said to myself: I should never have let him get away with it . . .

(ELSIE heaves a sigh and the bells jingle.)

. . . I should never have let him . . . (jingle) . . . I should never . . . (jingle). What's that jingling? I hear it! I hear it! It's my hat. Where are you? My hat! My hat! Where are you? My hat? Oh, Clever Elsie.

ELSIE: What?

PETER: My hat. Come on, Elsie.

ELSIE: Clever Elsie's indoors with Smiling John.

PETER: What?

ELSIE: He says so.

PETER: Who says so?

ELSIE: Smiling John says so.

PETER: Oh come on, my hat!

(Pause.)

ELSIE: There's something about this I don't understand.

PETER: My hat!

ELSIE: Let's talk about this. You like some beer?

PETER: You got some beer?

ELSIE: You say I'm My Hat. I'm not Elsie, 'cos
Elsie's at home with Smiling John. I must be
My Hat. Have a bit of cheese.

PETER: Smiling John says Clever Elsie's at home
with him, does he?

(They pass the beer to and fro, becoming pleasantly
giggly.)

PETER (singing):

Mrs Biggs, she had some pigs,

She fed them all on leather.

One went oink! (nudge in ribs)

The other went oink! (nudge in ribs)

They all went oink together! (He gestures with both
hands as if lifting a hat from his head to hers.)

ELSIE: I want to! I want to!

(He teaches her song and gestures. He wants her
to give him the hat. She keeps on fruitlessly
repeating his gesture at the end of the song until
she gets the idea and sets the bell hat on his head.
Repeat song. At the end, when he's not expecting it,
she puts the hat back on her own head. Repeat song,
this time he gets the hat back. Repeat song, at the
end she reaches for the hat but he holds on to it.

60

JOHN hears the music outside. Comes out of
house.)

JOHN: Clever Elsie! Clever Elsie! Is that you?

ELSIE: Smiling John!

JOHN: Who's that?

ELSIE: My hat.

JOHN: Clever Elsie! Clever Elsie!

ELSIE: He's lost Clever Elsie. I'd best go and help
him find her.

(PETER blows out lantern. ELSIE goes into house
and starts to look. PETER trips up in the dark.)

ELSIE: Clever Elsie! Clever Elsie! Where are you?
That's funny, she's not here.

(She sits.)

JOHN (hearing bells): Clever Elsie! I can hear you!
Clever Elsie!

(He stalks the bells. They search for each other
in the dark, i.e. in full light, the actors pretend
they cannot see each other.)

Ah! Ha ha!

(He grabs at sound and gets hat.)

Who's that?

PETER: Nobody!

(PETER escapes and exits.)

JOHN: Nobody? (looking at hat) Nobody's run off with
Clever Elsie . . . Nobody's run off with Clever
Elsie.

(JOHN goes back to house. Enters, sees ELSIE.)

Nobody's run off with Clever Elsie.

61

ELSIE: Where d'you get the hat?

JOHN: It's my hat.

ELSIE: That's right. (sets food, they eat) You sell the
sheep?

(JOHN lays notes on table. ELSIE rises and puts
money in a pot. Sits. They eat.)
Tomorrow we'll cut the hay. Saturday we'll go to
the fair . . . both of us.

(Pause. JOHN stops eating.)

JOHN: My hat! Fancy Nobody running off with a silly
girl like Clever Elsie.

(ELSIE goes on eating.)

A GOOD THING OR A BAD THING

NOTES

The audience should be encouraged to join in this play
and so there will be much ad libbing, especially during
the first half. However, the actors would be wise not
to mess about too much with the tightly structured
scenes (e.g. the first Queen scene and the 2 cottage
scenes) nor with certain rhythmic 'phrases' in scenes
which otherwise are fairly free (e.g. the first finding
of the gold button). Such return to structure requires
that the audience be quiet and this rests the children
and prevents over-excitement; it also provides points
at which the actors can combine to regain control.

MOTHER was played by a man in the first production.
While this perhaps weakens the message of the play
it allows five actors to cover two plays and adds much
fun.

JACK and MOTHER

JACK: Hello.

MUM: Hello.

JACK: You come to see the monster?

MOTHER: You seen it? Where is it?

JACK: You seen the monster, eh?

MOTHER: It's all safe, isn't it?

JACK: Oh Mum! It's in its cage. All those knights
captured it and brought it back here and locked
it up in a cage for us all to see.

MOTHER: Well, where is it? They say it's as big as
a house - bigger.

JACK (seeing something on ground): Hey!

MOTHER: What!

JACK: Look!

MOTHER: Where?

JACK: A gold button.

MOTHER: Oh don't do things like that. What a shock
you give me, I thought it was the monster.

JACK: Ain't it lovely. All twinkly.

MOTHER: That's not a button.

JACK: Not a button?

66

MOTHER: No holes.

JACK: No what?

MOTHER: No holes. You've got to have holes in a
button - to sew it on.

JACK: I wonder what it is? All shiny and round.

MOTHER: Well, it's not a button.

JACK: Any of you know what this is? You ever seen
anything like it before? . . . Round and gold . . .
and sort of . . .

(CHILDREN suggest 'money', 'sovereign'.)

MOTHER: A sovereign!

JACK: A sovereign!

(They confer whispering.)

What's it worth, a sovereign, anybody know? . . .
they say it's worth a 100p.

MOTHER (shouting): A 100p! (whispering) A 100p?

JACK: What are we going to do with it?

MOTHER: Hide it. Keep it.

JACK: It must belong to someone.

(MONSTER roar, off. The MONSTER is of course
always invisible; either offstage or imagined. JACK
and MOTHER retreat. JACK stuffs gold piece in
his pocket.)

MOTHER: The monster! Not here! Not right here!
(to CHILDREN) You never said it was right here.
Where is it? I thought it was in its cage.

JACK: There it is. There's its cage.

MOTHER: Is that a cage? It's so big. No wonder I
didn't see it. It looks like six double decker buses.

JACK: The monster's so big. They got to have a big
  cage.

MOTHER: Don't go too close.

JACK: There's plenty of bars.

MOTHER: It might get a paw through.

JACK: Can you see it, children? Lean forward . . .
  There.

MOTHER: It's all hair . . . and scales.

JACK: Can you see how big it is?

MOTHER: All matted. Look at its claws.

JACK: It's like a - it's like a - What d'you think it's
  like?

MOTHER: Slime.

JACK: Can you imagine a monster? What's it like?
  Big, d'you think? (ad lib) How big? Our monster's
  bigger than that. Your monster got sharp teeth?
  So's ours. Is your monster like a dragon, or a
  lion? Ours is like a huge gorilla, or maybe a
  dinosaur . . . it depends which side you look at
  it.

MOTHER: Look at its mouth, all slobber. What's that
  red stuff on its claws?

JACK: Blood.

MOTHER: Blood!

JACK: The monster used to live in the forest - remembe
  The great forest so big you could lose your way and
  never be seen again. They say the monster was
  there for a reason, a magic pool or something,
  guarding it. And a few people tried to get to the

pool and the monster killed them, and everyone
said something must be done. And so all the knights
went out, an army of them. The monster didn't
have a chance. They brought it back here and put
it in the cage for us all to see.

MOTHER: It's gone all quiet.

JACK: Sleepy. Shall I give it a poke?

MOTHER: Don't mess about with monsters.

> (JACK pokes. Terrific roar. They rush away.)

I told you not.

JACK: Give it a bit of chocolate.

MOTHER: D'you think we - ?

JACK: Oh go on. Here. (takes chocolate from MOTHER
and throws it) . . . It liked that.

MOTHER: Went down all in one go.

JACK: Did you like it then? Was it nice? Nice choccy?

MONSTER: Argh.

> (Bee buzzing round MOTHER, who swats it.)

JACK: Did you enjoy that then? No. I haven't got any
more.

> (Bee transfers to JACK, then MONSTER.)

Geroff . . .

MONSTER: Argh argh.

JACK: He's afraid of that bee. He's scared stiff.

MOTHER: He's cowering.

MONSTER: Argh!

JACK: It's been stung!

MONSTER: Argh argh.

JACK: Stung on its paw.

69

MONSTER: Argh.

JACK: Poor thing.

MOTHER: Be careful.

JACK: It wants some sympathy. It won't hurt me.

MONSTER (piteous): Argh.

JACK (pulling handkerchief from his pocket): I'll
    bandage its paw with my - oh!

MOTHER: What?

JACK: There!

MOTHER: Where? Ow!

JACK: Blast! It's rolled into the cage. My gold thing,
    my sovereign. I put it in my pocket and when I
    pulled out my - it rolled into the cage.

MOTHER: I said to give it to me.

JACK: Can I have my sovereign back please?

MONSTER (insouciant): Argh argh argh.

JACK: Finders isn't keepers if you know who the owner
    is - is it, children? Go on, tell him. Please can I
    have my sovereign back?

MONSTER (crafty): Argh argh.

JACK: What you want? You had the chocolate.

MOTHER: Leave him alone. Let it be.

JACK: Go on, be a sport, give us it back.

MOTHER: Silly old sovereign, who wants an old
    sovereign anyway?

JACK: Well what do you want?

MOTHER: Wish we'd never set eyes on the thing.

MONSTER: Argh argh argh argh.

JACK: I can't do that.

MONSTER: Argh argh argh.

JACK: You know I can't.

MONSTER: Argh.

MOTHER: All this fuss about a sovereign.

MONSTER: Argh argh argh argh.

MOTHER: What's he on about?

JACK: What you're asking is out of the question.

MONSTER: Argh.

JACK: Wants me to open the cage.

MOTHER: What!

JACK: Wants me to open the cage. Says it'll hand the
    sovereign out.

MOTHER: You can't do that. He can't do that.

MONSTER: Argh.

JACK: There's no need to get huffy. (pause) What you're
    asking is totally unreasonable.

MOTHER: Totally unreasonable.

JACK: You were put in that cage to keep you out of the
    way.

MOTHER: Think of all those people it ate.

JACK: Think of all those people you ate.

MONSTER (plausible): Argh argh argh argh argh.

JACK: All a misunderstanding, he says.

MOTHER: A likely tale.

MONSTER (Uriah Heep): Argh argh argh argh.

JACK: Well . . .

MONSTER: Argh argh argh.

JACK: If you faithfully promise . . .

MONSTER: Argh argh.

MOTHER: I wouldn't trust him.

JACK: D'you swear?

MONSTER: Argh.

MOTHER: Look at those claws.

JACK: What do you say, children? Shall I trust him
not to come out if I open the cage? . . . The
children say I shouldn't trust you. They think you
won't keep your promise.

MONSTER (injured innocence): Argh.

JACK: I would like my gold sovereign. Will you promise
not to come out? Just hand the sovereign through
the door?

MONSTER: Argh.

(JACK mimes opening the cage. Terrific roar.
JACK swept aside and dragged off.)

MOTHER: Hi! You! Stop! Hi! The monster's gone off
with our Jack. I told him not to open that cage. I
told him . . . He must have taken him off into the
forest. The forest! Nobody ever gets out of there
alive! . . . I'd better go after him . . . He'll never
manage without me . . . You come with me, will
you? . . . Let's go . . . Shall we go? . . . Off to
the forest? . . . Dark, isn't it? I can't see through
all those trees, can you? I wonder which way they
went? . . . I wish it wasn't so creepy . . . and
quiet . . . Oh I'm so glad I've got you for company,
I'm ever so glad you're with me. We're not scared,
are we? We're not scared . . . Aah! . . . It's a
broken branch . . . oh, that frightened me . . .

72

Did it frighten you? . . . Look, it's all trampled
here, and broken . . . why d'you think it's all
trampled? . . . D'you think the monster went
this way? . . . Let's go and see . . . Jack . . .
Jack . . . (going) Jack . . . Jack . . . .
(Exit MOTHER. MONSTER noises. Enter JACK,
his hands and feet tied. His hair is completely
covered by a woolly cap. The third finger of his
left hand is gold.)

JACK (speech punctuated by monster noises): All right,
all right, all right. What if I did fall in? It's not
my fault I fell asleep. It's only a mouldy old
pool . . . I said it's only a goldy old pool. Look
at it. Deep? I'll say its deep. You can't see the
bottom. All right, all right, I won't let anything
fall in again.
(MONSTER noises recede.)
Mouldy old pool.
(Enter MOTHER.)

MOTHER: Jack! Jack! We're here, all of us.

JACK: The children too?

MOTHER: Yes.
(MONSTER noises.)

JACK: The monster's coming back! Quick! Quick!
Hide! Pretend to be trees and bushes! Go on,
pretend to be trees and bushes.
(MONSTER noises loud, JACK nonchalant.)

JACK: Yes, yes, no. No one's been here. No, all right.
(MONSTER noises recede.)

73

All right, you can come out now. Get my hands
untied, he'll be back directly.

MOTHER: What if it comes back before I've got you
untied?

JACK: We'll have to think of something that'll scare
him. Can you think of anything that scares monsters?

MOTHER: Children! Can you think of anything that
scares monsters?

(CHILDREN will suggest 'Bees'.)

JACK: Bees! That's it! All make bee noises.

JACK & MOTHER: . . . suppose you all pretend to be
a swarm of bees. The monster'll hear you and he'll
be so scared of being stung that it'll give us time to
get away. You will help, won't you? Right, all you've
got to do is go Bzzzzz. Let's try it . . . Bzzzzzzzz
. . . well, I think it'll have to be a bit louder than
that, that won't scare the monster . . . Right,
let's have it again . . . bzzzzzzz. That's much
better but I'm sure if you really try you can make
it even louder. One last time, and really go bzzzzz.
Right. BZZZZZ, that's marvellous. Wonderful.
Right, when I tell you.

(MOTHER & JACK encourage children to make
bee noises. This can be developed into 'The girls
are doing better than the boys' etc.)

JACK: Now let's get these knots undone.

MOTHER (struggling): Oh I'm no good with knots. (to
CHILDREN) Any of you good with knots?

(Get two children out to help.)

74

MOTHER: I'll just go and see . . .

    (They listen.)

JACK: Mother! Keep back! You don't want to be eaten.

MOTHER: Eaten?

JACK: See these bones.

MOTHER: Bones?

JACK: There on the ground, by the pool.

MOTHER: That's twigs. White twigs.

JACK: Bones. Of people.

MOTHER: Eaten by the monster?

JACK: That's right.

MOTHER: Why didn't he eat you?

JACK: Fattening me up.

MOTHER: Fa -

JACK: Ssh!

MOTHER: Your finger!

JACK: Ssh. (pause) He's not far off.

MOTHER: What you done to your finger? It's all gold.

JACK: So's my hair.

MOTHER: Jack!

JACK: Ssh! You see the pool down there?

MOTHER: Is that the magic pool?

JACK: The monster set me to guard it. He didn't want
    anything falling in the water, no twigs, or leaves,
    or anything. Didn't want it polluted he said, didn't
    want it dirty. He didn't say why. Well, sitting there
    by the pool I got sort of sleepy and I wobbled a bit
    and sort of fell over, and I put out my hand to save
    myself and one finger splashed in the water . . .

75

and well . . .

MOTHER: Will it come off?

JACK: Don't think so.

MOTHER: Try a Brillo Pad when we get home.

JACK: Then I wanted to know what was in this pool.

MOTHER: I bet.

JACK: I leaned over the water and two hairs from my
head fell in . . . and they turned gold.

MOTHER: Never!

JACK: Then I couldn't help it - I wanted to see - I had
to try - I dipped my whole head in the pool, and
now look at it.

(Pause.)

MOTHER: I must say -

JACK: I am a fool.

MOTHER: It looks lovely. A real treat.

JACK: It's daft.

MOTHER: Don't cover it up.

JACK: I feel silly. What I want to go and do a daft thing
like that for?

MOTHER: It's lovely! (to children) Oh yes it is!
(Develop 'Oh no it isn't' etc.)

JACK: Wait a minute.

MOTHER: Is it coming back?

JACK: I think so.

(MONSTER noises.)

We'd better get out of here. Come on it's getting
nearer.

MOTHER: The children'll help us.

JACK: Will you pretend to be bees again? Scare the
monster off while we run away? Wait till I give the
signal . . . Ready. Now! BZZZZZ.
(Loud MONSTER noises. Exit MOTHER and JACK.)

COTTAGE
(MOTHER brings food.)
MOTHER: Here's your tea.
(Enter JACK; he wears a cap to hide his hair. Also
a fine new pair of boots, which his MOTHER doesn't
see.)
I wish you'd take that cap off.
JACK: It's my hair.
MOTHER: I don't know why you're so silly about it.
JACK: Folks stare at me.
MOTHER: It looks nice.
JACK: Oh . . .
MOTHER: You still getting on all right with Mr. Trevor?
JACK (eating): Mm.
MOTHER: He pleased with you? You learn all you can
from Mr. Trevor.
JACK: Mm.
MOTHER: Maybe one day you'll be head gardener your-
self . . . We're all right, but we could do with a bit
more . . . I sometimes think of those bones.
JACK: Bones?
MOTHER: If we'd dipped a few in the pond - we'd be rich.
We're all right as we are. We got a home. You got
a good job.

77

JACK: I wish I'd killed that monster.

MOTHER: Just as well you didn't try.

JACK: I wish I'd got a sword.

MOTHER: What nonsense.

JACK: I'd run him through.

MOTHER: I won't have talk like that, you hear? I won't have it. We were lucky to get away. It was only thanks to the children. No one else has ever got away from that monster. Not alone they haven't.

JACK: Still around, though. Killing people. Wish I'd got a sword.

MOTHER: I don't want you getting killed and hurt . . . I don't want them bringing you home all hurt. (She sees boots.) Wherever did you get them?

JACK: What?

MOTHER: Those.

JACK: Lady give me them.

MOTHER: A lady give you them!

JACK: Yeah. She come into the garden.

MOTHER: She come into the - !

JACK: She come into the garden and give me them.

MOTHER: I don't believe you.

JACK: It's true!

MOTHER: You stole them.

JACK: I didn't!

MOTHER: We got a nice cottage -

JACK: I did not.

MOTHER: You got a steady job -

JACK: I did not steal them.

78

MOTHER: Gardener's boy to Mr. Trevor.

JACK: Mother!

MOTHER: Be head gardener yourself some day.

JACK: A lady give me them.

(Pause.)

MOTHER: What sort of lady? What she look like, this lady

JACK: I dunno.

MOTHER: Well, was she short or tall?

JACK: I dunno.

MOTHER: Was she pretty?

JACK: Pretty?

MOTHER: Yes, pretty.

JACK: I dunno.

MOTHER: How old was she?

JACK: How should I know? . . . She wore a crown.

MOTHER: A crown! . . .

JACK: Well -

MOTHER: The Queen . . . ! The Queen give you a pair
of boots? Let's see them.

JACK: I dunno it was the Queen, do I? She never said.

MOTHER: I'm sure they're very nice boots. Ever so
fine. I wonder why she give them to you?

GARDEN

(JACK working. QUEEN.)

QUEEN: Good morning.

JACK: Oh, good morning, ma'am. Your Majesty.

QUEEN: Why don't you take your cap off?

JACK: What? I - er - pardon?

79

QUEEN: You should take off your cap when you speak
     to a lady.

JACK: Oh, I . . . er . . . I don't like . . .

QUEEN: Take it off. (an order) Take it off.
     (JACK does so.)
     There. There.

JACK: I wish you wouldn't look at me like that.

QUEEN: You are the boy to whom I gave the boots.

JACK: I'm just the gardener's boy.

QUEEN: I'm just the gardener's boy! (pause) What is
     your name?

JACK: John, but I'm called Jack. Can I put my cap on?

QUEEN: No. Who calls you Jack?

JACK: My mother.

QUEEN: You live with your mother?

JACK: Yes.

QUEEN: No one else?

JACK: Who else would there be? . . . Can I put my -

QUEEN: No. (pause) Do you like your boots?

JACK: They're all right.

QUEEN: Would you like something else that's nice to wear

JACK: I don't mind.

QUEEN: Don't be so sulky. Beautiful. It's pleasant to
     make beautiful things more beautiful. I shall give you
     a cloak.

JACK: I'd like a sword.

QUEEN: Oh, so he'd like a sword. And why would you
     like a sword?

JACK: To kill the monster.

QUEEN (laughs): Oh my little hero! No one will ever
     kill the monster. The monster kills them. No one
     dare go into the forest since it escaped.
JACK: Give me a sword and I shall kill the monster.
QUEEN: If I give you a sword will you give me a kiss?
     (slight pause) You can put on your cap. (going) No
     one will ever kill the monster. He eats them all.
     (Exit QUEEN. JACK replaces cap.)

COTTAGE
     (MOTHER. Enter JACK wearing boots and sword.)
JACK: The monster's carried off the princess!
MOTHER: The princess?
JACK: The monster. He's carried her off.
MOTHER: Poor thing.
JACK: Came in the night. No one heard.
MOTHER: Her poor mother.
JACK: Smashed down a door. Stuck an arm through a
     window.
MOTHER: She's barely sixteen.
JACK: There's a reward for whoever gets her back.
MOTHER: Here's your tea. A reward?
JACK: They can marry her.
MOTHER: I kept it hot.
JACK: Don't want anything.
MOTHER: Come on now, eat it up.
JACK: I want to go, Mother.
MOTHER: That's enough of that.
JACK: I want to kill the monster.

MOTHER: I never heard such nonsense. Eat up your
    tea.
JACK: I got boots. I got a sword.
MOTHER: You stay here and look after your mother.
JACK: You and I - we been there. We know. We know
    about the way, the place, the pool. We know. We're
    the only ones that've been and got back.
MOTHER: Thanks to them.
    (Pause.)
JACK: I'm going, Mother. (pause) Mother.
MOTHER: I'll come with you.
JACK: I've got to go by myself.
MOTHER: I could help find the way.
JACK: No.
MOTHER: Rushing off after monsters when you're
    perfectly well off here. Got a perfectly good job.
    Let me give your sword a shine. Try and eat
    something. Remember not to get your feet wet.
    Here, take this with you. Take a spare pair of
    socks. If you feel a cold coming on take some
    vitamin C. Where's your muffler? . . . Look
    after yourself, son.

FOREST
(JACK draws his sword. Listens. Creeps from
tree to tree. PRINCESS.)
JACK: It's the princess . . . I'd forgotten all about
    her . . . psst . . . pssst . . . psst -
PRINCESS: Who's that?

82

JACK: Me. I've come to rescue you.

PRINCESS: Oh. Who are you?

JACK: Jack. The gardener's boy. Fattening you up,
   was he?

PRINCESS: I thought it would be a knight.

JACK: Where is it?

PRINCESS: What?

JACK: The monster.

PRINCESS: Gone off to kill a few people. Well, untie
   my hands. If you rescue me I'll have to marry
   you.

JACK: Oh, I just came to kill the monster.
   (JACK starts to drag across some pieces of wood.)

PRINCESS: What are you doing?

JACK: Covering up the pond.

PRINCESS: Covering up the pond?

JACK: Hiding it, making a trap.

PRINCESS: Why don't we get away while there's still
   time?

JACK: Monster comes, doesn't see pond, comes after
   us. Falls in.

PRINCESS (after a moment's hesitation): Here, let
   me help.

JACK: Thanks. Now some of that light stuff. Not
   enough to hold him up, just hide it.
   (MONSTER approaching.)
   There it is. Come on, over here.
   (They stand on the far side of the pond and taunt
   the MONSTER. MONSTER noises get immensely

(loud. Huge crash. JACK and PRINCESS pile chairs, tables, anything on top of pool. Then sit on it themselves. Subterranean monster noises. JACK and PRINCESS exhausted. PRINCESS's hands are gold.)

JACK: Thanks.

PRINCESS: That's all right. I quite enjoyed it.

JACK: Couldn't have done it without you.

PRINCESS (seeing her hands. Terrified) Ah!

JACK: What's - ? Don't be frightened. It's all right. You must have splashed them. Look I've got a finger . . . and my hair . . . it's the pool. It turns things into gold.

PRINCESS: Won't it come off?

JACK: No . . . It's better than being eaten . . . It's quite pretty really, anyway your hands are pretty.

PRINCESS: Your hair is lovely.

JACK: I used to think it was silly.

PRINCESS: No . . . It's lovely.

(Pause.)

JACK: We're two of a kind.

(Pause.)

PRINCESS: Yes . . . You're a lot cleverer than any of the knights I know, and kinder.

(Pause.)

What happens now?

JACK: Kill him.

PRINCESS: How are you going to get at him?

(JACK cautiously lifts a bit of wood.)

MONSTER: Argh!

84

JACK (quickly replaces wood): Did you see his eye?

PRINCESS: Yes.

JACK: I'll run him through the eye with my sword.

PRINCESS: It seems a waste to kill him. It could be quite useful having a monster around.

JACK: You barmy?

PRINCESS: If he promised to behave and serve you.

JACK: I've had some of his promises. The children can tell you how he keeps his promises.

MONSTER: Argh argh!

JACK: Oh no. You're going to be killed.

PRINCESS: It's different now. You're different.

JACK: What if he starts roaming round the world again looking for people to eat?

PRINCESS: It's easy to kill monsters. The sensible thing is to control them and make them work for you. This monster knows you're cleverer than he is, so he'll always obey you.

MONSTER: Argh!

JACK (ironic): Oh ho ho. And what if he doesn't obey me?

PRINCESS: You clobber him and put him back in his hole.

JACK: He's bigger than me.

PRINCESS: But you're cleverer . . . Hey! You down there! You listening?

MONSTER: Argh.

PRINCESS: You heard what we been saying. Do you agree?

MONSTER: Argh argh.

PRINCESS: You stay down there till Jack here calls you and then you come and do as he says.

MONSTER: Argh.

PRINCESS: And then go back down into your pond.

MONSTER (extremely suspect): Argh.

JACK: I don't trust that monster an inch. What do you think, children? Should I kill it or not? Hands up those who think I ought to kill the monster . . . Hands up those who think I ought to keep the monster alive . . . There, you see?

PRINCESS: Let me show you. Let's try it both ways. (to MONSTER) No funny tricks now or he'll clobber you. Right. We'll try it both ways! What happens if you kill the monster and what if you don't. Let's go back to the palace.

JACK: Have we got to meet your mother? . . . What do I do? Do I bow?

PRINCESS: Yes, or you can kneel, she likes that, it makes her happy.

JACK: It makes her happy.

PRINCESS: It makes her very happy. (Exit. Immediately enter QUEEN followed by JACK and PRINCESS.)

QUEEN: Swaggering! Bumptious! Outrageous! Impudent!

PRINCESS: Mama!

QUEEN: Presumptuous! Overweening! (JACK trips over his sword and ends up kneeling.) Why's he not kneeling?

PRINCESS: He is kneeling.

QUEEN: Where's his cap?

PRINCESS: His cap?

QUEEN: Yes, his cap. He doesn't like his hair.

PRINCESS: He does like his hair.

(Pause.)

QUEEN: Do you like your hair?

JACK: Yes.

QUEEN: Guard! Guard! Off with his head!

(Exit QUEEN.)

JACK: What?

PRINCESS: You heard.

JACK: But I'll be dead.

PRINCESS: Now do you see? . . . But if we'd had the
    monster . . . Let's try, this time we'll try and see
    what happens if you've got the monster. Right?

JACK: Right.

(Enter QUEEN.)

QUEEN: A gardener's boy! Marry my daughter! The
    reward was intended for an honourable knight.

PRINCESS: What's honour anyway? Just a set of rules!

JACK: Honour's not a bad thing in itself.

QUEEN: Who told you to speak?

PRINCESS: What if you end up dead?

JACK: There's worse things than dying.

QUEEN: Listen to me!

PRINCESS: I'm going to marry him.

JACK: I rescued her.

PRINCESS: He's clever and kind.

JACK: She's beautiful.

QUEEN: A gardener's boy!

JACK: Shall we try it?

PRINCESS: Yes.

QUEEN: A lout in boots!

JACK: What if it won't go back?

QUEEN: An oaf with a sword!

PRINCESS: You'll be dead anyway!

QUEEN: Marry my daughter!

JACK: Shall we?

PRINCESS: We must.

QUEEN: Guard!

JACK: Monster!

QUEEN: Guard! Guard!

JACK: Monster!

QUEEN: Off with his head!

JACK: To your master!

(Growing MONSTER noises.)

QUEEN: Guard! Gu -

(All retreat before MONSTER. JACK as lion tamer.)

JACK: Back! Back! Down, you brute! Down I say! Down, sir!

PRINCESS: Now we've only to say: 'Monster eat Queen' and nothing on earth can save you.

QUEEN (angry): Ah!

MONSTER: Argh.

JACK: I wouldn't do that if I were you.

MONSTER: Argh.

JACK: Don't try him too hard. I've barely got him under

88

control.

PRINCESS: Mama, may we or may we not get married?
(Exit QUEEN.)
You see! Now if we hadn't had the monster . . .

JACK: We are left with one tiny problem.

PRINCESS: What's that?

JACK: Do you know what it is, children . . . ? That's
right. How to get him back in his hole.

PRINCESS: Tell him to go.

JACK: Just tell him?

PRINCESS: Yes, just tell him.

JACK (clearing his throat): Hm. Back you go now into
your hole.
(Pause.)
Off you go into your hole. (pause) Into your hole.

MONSTER: Argh.

PRINCESS: Act nonchalant. Pretend you're not worried.

JACK: What are we going to do?

MONSTER: Argh argh.

JACK: I've got it! Let's get the children to help.

PRINCESS: Yes.

JACK: All of you. Remember last time? Being a swarm
of bees, how frightened the monster was? You
pretend to be a swarm of bees again and buzz him
back like you did before. Right now! Bzzzz.
Louder!

PRINCESS: Louder! Louder!
Bzzzzzzzz
Bzzzzzzzz

89

QUEEN MARGARET COLLEGE LIBRARY

Bzzzzzzzz

(Exit MONSTER.)

JACK: Whew! Well, on balance I suppose you're right. It might be a good idea to have him around. He's dangerous but he's powerful. I just hope that next time we want to let him out the children are here to help us get him back.

PRINCESS: I tell you what: you only let him out when they're all here.

JACK: That's it. The monster only comes out when all the children are here to help us get him back.

PRINCESS: Bye bye.

JACK: Bye bye - and thanks.

QUEEN ELIZABETH
CENTRAL
STUDENT LIBRARY
PHYSIOTHERAPY
DISTRICT.

CANCELLED

CANCELLED

SOFT TISSUE INJURIES IN SPORT

FOR PETER, ROBIN, HELEN & MICHAEL

Soft Tissue Injuries
in Sport

SYLVIA LACHMANN

MA, MB, BChir, MRCP
Senior Medical Officer
Disabilities Services Association
of the Department of Health and Social Security
Cambridge Artificial Limb and Appliance Centre
Honorary Consultant in Rehabilitation
Addenbrooke's Hospital Cambridge

Blackwell Scientific Publications
OXFORD LONDON EDINBURGH BOSTON PALO ALTO MELBOURNE

© 1988 by
Blackwell Scientific Publications
Editorial offices:
Osney Mead, Oxford OX2 0EL
  (*Orders*: Tel. 0865-240201)
8 John Street, London WC1N 2ES
23 Ainslie Place, Edinburgh EH3 6AJ
3 Cambridge Center, Suite 208, Cambridge, Massachusetts 02142, USA
667 Lytton Avenue, Palo Alto, California 94301, USA
107 Barry Street, Carlton, Victoria 3053, Australia

All rights reserved. No part of this
publication may be reproduced, stored
in a retrieval system, or transmitted,
in any form or by any means,
electronic, mechanical, photocopying,
recording or otherwise without
the prior permission of the
copyright owner

First published 1988

Set by Times Graphics Singapore

Printed in the UK by Butler and Tanner Ltd Frome & London

DISTRIBUTORS

USA
  Year Book Medical Publishers
  200 North LaSalle Street, Chicago, Illinois 60601
  (*Orders*: Tel. 312-726-9733)

Canada
  The C.V. Mosby Company
  5240 Finch Avenue East, Scarborough, Ontario
  (*Orders*: Tel. 416-298-1588)

Australia
  Blackwell Scientific Publications (Australia) Pty Ltd
  107 Barry Street, Carlton, Victoria 3053
  (*Orders*: Tel. 03-347-0300)

British Library
Cataloguing in Publication Data

Lachmann, Sylvia
  Soft tissue injuries in sport.
  1. Sports — Accidents and injuries
  I. Title
  617'.1027   RD97

  ISBN 0-632-01964-6

1785508 X

Contents

Preface

This book is based on 9 years' experience of running a Sports Injury Clinic. During this time over 6000 patients, the majority with soft tissue injuries, have walked or limped through the doorway. I hope this book will be of use to doctors and physiotherapists working in similar clinics, to general practitioners, team doctors and physiotherapists and to medical and physiotherapy students. I think it may also be useful to coaches and some athletes. An appreciation of body mechanisms and responses not only helps an individual to respond appropriately to injury and to comply with recommended treatment regimes, but may help to avert potential injuries, or to prevent acute injuries becoming chronic. Coaches training junior athletes need to know how immature tissues respond to mechanical stresses in order to avoid permanent damage and deformity.

As a rheumatologist I am interested in soft tissue inflammation. Whether this is initiated by immunological or traumatic insults, the subsequent tissue responses are similar. I believe an understanding of events at cellular and tissue level is important when planning and carrying out treatment.

In Section I of the book the basic structure of the connective tissues is described, and the mechanisms and progress of tissue damage, inflammation and repair explained. This is followed by an account of how these processes can be influenced, for better or worse, by external factors such as physiotherapy and drugs. The differing responses of various tissues (muscle, ligament and tendon) to trauma are then given and appropriate treatments outlined in general terms.

Section II deals with the diagnosis and management of specific injuries under headings of different body parts, starting with the feet and moving upwards.

I would like to take this opportunity of thanking the Institute of Sports Medicine, The University of Cambridge and its Colleges, and the Peter Wilson Memorial Fund of the Daily Mirror for financial help with setting up and running the clinic.

Finally many thanks are due to the doctors, physiotherapists and clerical staff who have devoted so much time and enthusiasm to the clinic.

Sylvia Lachmann

Section I

General Considerations

1

Introduction

This book is primarily about the management of soft tissue injuries as seen in a Sports Injury Clinic, and is intended for use by the staff of such clinics and those responsible for the well-being of athletes. Brief mention is made of other topics that sometimes may be raised by the patients, such as some systemic effects of exertion. The staff of a Sports Injury Clinic may be asked to help organise a sporting event, and there is a short section on the importance of environmental conditions.

For the most part, the patients are 'walking wounded', since the more serious injuries, such as fractures, head and eye injuries, would go straight to the Accident and Emergency Service. The injuries are mainly soft tissue, i.e. muscles, ligaments and tendons, with some joint problems and the occasional unsuspected fracture. The majority of the injuries are to the lower limbs (see Table 1.1).

The prevalence of the sports causing the injuries varies from place to place, depending on what is popular locally. At the Cambridge Sports Injury Clinic, the frequencies of different sports causing injuries is shown in Table 1.2. The position of a particular sport in this table depends on several factors, the most important of which are the number of people participating in the sport, and the injury rate for that sport.

The aim of a Sports Injury Clinic is to see the injuries early, make an accurate diagnosis and institute prompt and appropriate treatment. With proper management, the majority of injuries recover completely, and the athlete returns to full activity. If injuries are not managed appropriately, they may become chronic with deleterious long-term changes in the tissues, which may cause prolonged

Table 1.1. Injuries attending the Cambridge Sports Injury Clinic

Sports injuries	Percentage	
Knee	27	
Foot and ankle	20	
Lower leg	15	
Thigh	14	Total 4 000
Lumbar region	10	
Arm and hand	8	
Trunk	4	
Head and neck	2	

Table 1.2. Sports causing injuries in descending frequency — series of 4 000 injuries

Sport	Percentage
Running	19
Soccer	18
Rugby	17
Rowing	10
Squash	7
Hockey	3
Badminton	2.5
Tennis	2.5
Cricket	2
Others	19

disability and even long-term changes such as osteoa...
changes affect not only the individual's sporting prowess...
ability to work and the general quality of life. Ideally the...
should be applied to the management of all soft tiss...
however caused.

Injuries may be divided into two groups — acute in...
overuse injuries. Either type, if mismanaged, may become ...
injury. It is very important to realise that the terms ove...
chronic injuries are not synonymous.

Acute injuries may be endogenous or exogenous, depen...
whether an external object is involved or not. Often the...
complex. Impact, twisting, friction, shearing or stretching...
may inflict the damage (see Fig. 1.1).

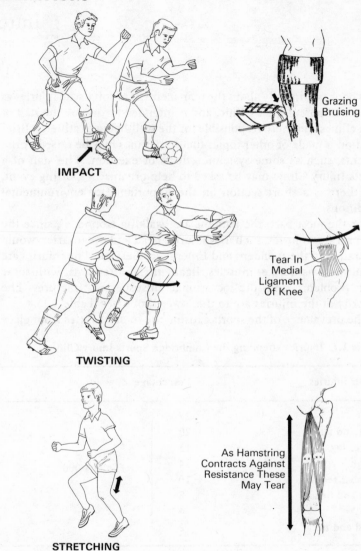

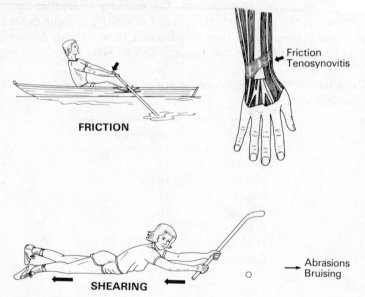

Fig. 1.1. Possible causes of soft tissue injuries.

4

Impact may be with another player, and injury is particularly likely from bony prominences such as knee, elbow or head, or if struck by the opponent's hard protective gear, e.g. boot or helmet. Apparatus in the form of balls, bats, sticks or racqets may cause the injury. On other occasions impact occurs with stationary objects such as goal posts, walls and fences, or a hard playing surface. Such injuries usually cause skin contusion or abrasion, with underlying haematomas which may be subdermal, intramuscular or subperiosteal.

Twisting injuries are common in contact sports, due to a tackle from another player, or to the individual's boot sticking during turning, as may occur on a muddy pitch. This puts rotational strains on ankle and knee particularly, and there is liable to be damage to ligaments and intra-articular structures. Such injuries can be reduced by ensuring players wear footwear appropriate for the condition of the playing surface.

Shearing forces are applied when part of the body is in contact with a surface, e.g. hand on oar, heel on counter of shoe, and results in abrasions or blisters. Friction within the body may occur between tendons, and their investing tendon sheath, if there is one, causing tenosynovitis, or with surrounding loose connective tissue causing peritendinitis.

Stretching injuries are most likely to occur when muscles are taut, such as early on if the pre-exercise warm-up has been inadequate, or when movements are unco-ordinated due to poor postural reflexes, or lack of skill, or when muscles are fatigued and the normal postural bio-feedback mechanisms fail. Intramuscular scar tissue from previous injuries may have contracted if it was not stretched regularly during healing and again during warm-up — such tight knots of scar tissue are particularly liable to tear. Usually the tear occurs in the muscle belly but occasionally it may be avulsed from the bony origin or tendinous insertion. Even more occasionally, a muscle or tendon may suffer a total rupture.

Overuse injuries are due to repetitive stresses on vulnerable tissues, and may have been developing over days or weeks, although they often come to notice acutely with a sudden onset of symptoms. They are associated with prolonged activities such as running, done either for its own sake or as training for other sports. Other prolonged events such as rowing, swimming, cycling and racquet sports also cause overuse injuries.

Repeated mechanical stress may disrupt the microstructure of tissues. Stress fractures in bone, and epiphyseal damage to the growing bones of adolescents are due to compressive forces. Repeated tugging may also cause damage — the enthesopathies are injuries where the insertion of muscle or fascia into the periosteum is tugged repeatedly, causing tearing of the insertion and lifting of the periosteum, and local inflammation, e.g. tennis elbow and medial shin splints. Repeated traction on tendons may cause degenerative changes inside the tendon. An example of this is degenerative cyst formation in the Achilles tendon. In children and adolescents, repetitive traction at epiphyses causes damage, e.g. Osgood–Schlatter disease of the tibial tubercle, or an apophysitis where the tendon is inserted into bone, e.g. Sever's disease of the calcaneum.

Recurrent awkward movements at joints may repeatedly stress ligaments, causing tearing of fibres with inflammation and even calcification. Breast-stroke swimmers used to suffer soreness of the medial collateral ligament of the knee due to a wide leg kick. When the cause of this was recognised by the governing body of the sport, the leg kick was made narrower, and this injury has now virtually disappeared. A similar injury occurs to the medial ligament of the elbow in javelin throwers who throw with a round elbow.

Some repetitive movements cause friction injuries. These may be of tendons such as tenosynovitis of wrist extensors in rowers and Achilles peritendinitis in runners. The snapping band syndrome is due to friction between the ilio-tibial tract and the lateral side of the knee joint. Bursitis at a variety of sites is due to friction either from tendons (e.g. trochanteric bursa underlying the gluteal tendons and subacromial bursa at the shoulder), or from external objects (e.g. retrocalcaneal bursitis due to friction from the back of the shoe). The pain and stiffness of the patello-femoral syndrome is due to friction between the back of the patella and the lower end of the femur.

Long-distance runners are particularly susceptible to overuse injuries, due to the repetitive footfall. Any minor skeletal abnormalities or malalignments are relevant as they put abnormal stresses on the skeletal frame. Variants from normal bony configuration of the feet or knees, rotation of the femur, discrepancies of leg length, are all magnified as a runner increases the weekly mileage, and these minor skeletal aberrations which would be insignificant during normal activity become increasingly likely to cause symptoms.

Chronic injuries usually develop because acute or overuse injuries are neglected or treated wrongly, so that instead of resolution and repair occurring, there is repeated damage and inflammation, causing a local accumulation of chronic scar tissue which remains vascular and painful, as it contains pain-sensitive nerve endings. This type of injury can be treated, and usually recovers, although treatment is often painful, and the response slow.

Long-term damage to joints may occur following ligament sprains. Correct treatment results in a strong ligament with a full range of joint movements, strong periarticular muscles and intact proprioceptive reflexes. Prolonged immobilisation or neglect may result in a stretched ligament, weak muscles and lost proprioceptive sense, so that the joint is poorly supported and suffers recurrent damage to ligaments and articular surfaces, which lead to changes indistinguishable from osteoarthritis.

Once a diagnosis is established, the treatment of soft tissue injuries relies on prompt, skilled and intensive physiotherapy. Only in some conditions is rest appropriate — in most cases early and carefully monitored mobilisation is needed. Non-steroidal anti-inflammatory drugs (NSAIDs) are often of great help. Treatment should be continued until the player can return to training. Any injuries requiring orthopaedic management should be referred without delay.

The Sports Injury Clinic has an educative role in helping players to understand how injuries happen, and how they may be avoided. If possible, the staff of a Sports Injury Clinic should circularise local sports clubs with some basic information about the prevention and first aid treatment of injuries. A format along the lines given in Table 1.3 is suitable.

This book is arranged so that Section I describes the microscopic structures of tissues and the processes of inflammation and repair: the effects of different treatments are described; the general characteristics of injuries to particular tissues are outlined, and mention is made of systemic reactions to exertion and environmental factors. In Section II specific injuries are described by body part.

Table 1.3. Prevention and treatment of minor sports injuries

Fitness	Training, preferably under supervision, increases flexibility and improves performance. If possible, start training 4–6 weeks before the season starts
Warm up	Muscles perform better and resist injury better when they are warm. Jogging and stretching exercises are best for a minimum period of 15 minutes, preferably in warm clothing, ending not more than 5 minutes before the event
Equipment	Should be suitable and in good condition, e.g. footwear, mouth guards, pads, jock straps, and gloves
Obey rules	Many of them are designed to prevent injury
Anti-tetanus and polio vaccinations	Make sure you have had them and have an anti-tetanus booster every 4–5 years

2
Connective Tissue, Inflammation and Repair

Some knowledge of the structure of soft tissues, and the processes of inflammation and repair is helpful in the clinical management of soft tissue injuries.

FIBROUS CONNECTIVE TISSUES

These tissues all consist of collagen fibres embedded in ground substance, both these components being formed by fibroblasts. The mature tissue typically contains few fibroblasts and some scattered histocytes. The blood supply is scanty. The fibres consist of collagen type I, which has great tensile strength. They form the dominant structural element. Varying dispositions of the fibres underly the different connective tissue structures.

Ligaments

Ligaments run from bone to bone, holding them together. They are frequently a thickened portion of the joint capsule, or separate and outside the capsule, for example lateral collateral ligaments of the knee, or the interspinous ligaments in the vertebral column.

Ligaments consist of dense bundles of collagen fibres running approximately parallel to the line of pull, but the bundles of fibres do interweave to some extent to form a mesh (see Fig. 2.1). They are usually flattened, and made up of several interconnected parallel sheets. Collagen is not extensible but a few ligaments contain some elastin, which renders them somewhat resilient, for instance the ligamentum flavum of the spine. A few flattened fibroblasts can be seen between the fibres. The blood supply is sparse and consists of small vessels running longitudinally.

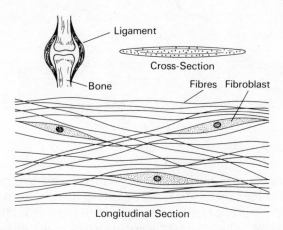

Fig. 2.1. Microscopic views of ligament.

Tendons

Tendons attach muscle to bone (see Fig. 2.2). They vary in length, and are usually round in cross section. The microscopic structure is similar to that of ligaments, except that the fibres run in parallel. They are very strong, the tensile strength being similar to that of bone.

Tendon sheaths

In some sites where the tendon runs over bone, or under retinaculum or ligamentous bands, there is a tendon sheath. This has two layers; an outer layer which is a connective tissue sheath attached to

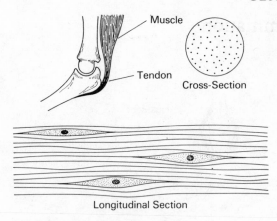

Fig. 2.2. Microscopic views of tendon.

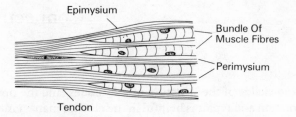

Fig. 2.3. Attachment of tendon to muscle.

Attachment of tendon to muscle

The collagen fibres diverge and surround the ends of the muscle fibre, and mingle with the collagen fibres of the epimysium (see Fig. 2.3).

Attachment of ligament or tendon to bone

In this case, the collagen fibres intermesh with the dense collagen fibres of the periosteum (see Fig. 2.4). If the tugging pulls the periosteum away from the bone, the osteoblasts will lay down new bone to fill the space, and in this way a spur may develop.

surrounding structures, and an inner sheath enclosing and being attached to the tendon. The space between the sheaths is normally minimal, and is filled with a fluid rich in hyaluronic acid similar to synovial fluid. There is no synovial membrane, the surfaces being covered largely with intercellular substance and the occasional synovial cell. This arrangement reduces friction, and allows the tendons to glide through surrounding tissues. Good examples are seen surrounding the tendons of the forearm muscles.

Bursae

Bursae are clefts in the connective tissue containing normally only a little fluid. They occur where ligaments or tendons cross bone or other structures, and prevent friction during movement, e.g. the trochanteric bursa cushions the tendon of glutei maximus and medius as it passes over the greater trochanter. Similar structures lie below the skin overlying bony structures, and serve a similar purpose; e.g. prepatellar bursa. When irritated more fluid is secreted, and they expand into fluid-filled sacs.

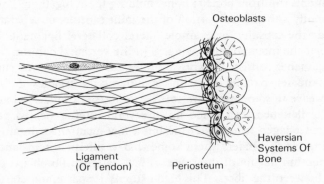

Fig. 2.4. Attachment of ligament or tendon to bone.

Attachment of ligament or tendon to cartilage

Collagen fibres extend into the cartilage forming a zone of fibrocartilage at the site of attachment. Rows of chondrocytes replace fibroblasts as the cellular element (see Fig. 2.5).

During growth of bone and cartilage, remodelling occurs at the site of attachment of the ligament or tendon, and the original insertion may become buried.

Aponeuroses

Aponeuroses are wide flattened sheets of collagen fibres by which muscles may attach to bone or fascia; e.g. the fascia lata of the thigh, and the bicipital aponeurosis of the forearm.

Deep fascia

Fascia consists of thin flat sheets of interweaving collagen fibres. In the limbs, the deep fascia is well developed into strong membranes

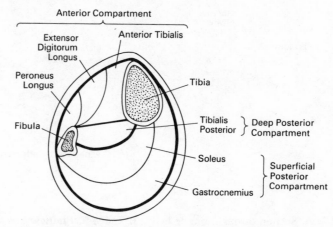

Fig. 2.6. Fascial compartments of the lower leg.

which surround muscles. These form a series of compartments, the walls of which give origin to muscle fibres (see Fig. 2.6). Sheets penetrate between muscle bellies and are attached to bone by their fibres becoming continuous with those of the periosteum. In the hands and feet, exceptionally thick fascia forms the palmar and plantar fasciae.

SKELETAL MUSCLE

Skeletal muscle is a very specialised form of connective tissue (see Fig. 2.7). The contractile striated fibres are cells up to 40 cm long; they contain many nuclei situated peripherally, and actin and myosin fibres which are contractile. The muscle fibres are supported and bound together by fibrous connective tissue. A delicate web of collagen surrounds individual fibres, the endomysium. These units are grouped into bundles by the perimysium and these in turn are retained by the epimysium which surrounds the whole muscle and

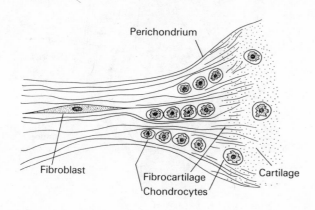

Fig. 2.5. Attachment of ligament or tendon to cartilage.

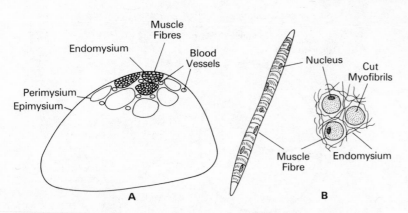

Fig. 2.7. A. Section through muscle belly. B. Individual muscle fibres.

blends with bone or tendon at the muscle origin and attachment. The epimysium has a smooth outer surface which means the muscle can move freely as it contracts and relaxes (see Fig 2.7A). Fibroblasts are scattered through the connective tissue. Muscle has a rich blood supply which ramifies through the supporting connective tissue, and supplies oxygen and nutrients to the fibres. The vessels dilate when the muscle is active.

The motor nerves carry efferent impulses stimulating contraction. Each motor neuron supplies a number of individual fibres scattered through the muscle — a motor unit. The motor units may consist of only a few fibres, or a great many, depending on the fineness of movement controlled by that muscle. The strength of contraction at any one time depends on how many motor units are firing. There are two different types of skeletal muscle fibre — Type I (slow) and Type II (fast). These have different enzymes and histological appearances. Put at its simplest, Type I fibres perform slow repetitive contractions concerned with maintaining posture, whilst Type II produce rapid movement but fatigue more easily. The distribution of fibre types in different muscles appears to reflect these functions.

The effect of training is to increase muscle bulk by increasing the size of individual fibres, and to improve function by recruiting more motor units. Loss of the nerve supply, disuse or inflammation in the adjacent joint all result in muscle astrophy.

JOINTS

A schematised synovial joint is represented in Fig. 2.8. The articular surfaces of the bones are covered by hyaline cartilage which is smooth and resilient. The joint is enclosed by a collagenous capsule and the inside of the capsule and non-articular surfaces of bone are covered with synovial membrane, the cells of which secrete synovial

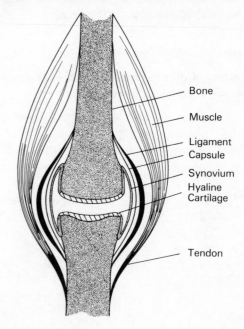

Fig. 2.8. Schematised joint.

10

fluid, which lubricates the surfaces. In a healthy joint, the quantity of fluid is small. The capsule may be thickened in places by ligaments, or the ligaments may run separately outside the capsule. The capsule itself is usually not very strong, and it is the ligaments which hold the bones in apposition. Muscles cross the joint and move it by contractions. The capsule, synovium and bone (but not the articular cartilage) contain sensory nerve endings. Bone has a rich blood supply, whilst cartilage is avascular.

Some joints contain fibrocartilage structures which together with the shape of the bone surfaces, influence movement, e.g. in the knee and temporomandibular joints.

PROPRIOCEPTIVE SYSTEM

There are a variety of receptors in joints, ligaments, tendons and muscles which respond to mechanical stress and movement, and impulses from these are supplemented from similar mechanoceptors in the skin.

Muscle spindles lie within muscles (Fig. 2.9A), and consist of modified muscle fibres which measure tension. The efferent fibres alter the degree of contraction in the fibres, and hence vary the 'setting'. The primary afferent fibres measure the degree and rate of stretch, and the secondary afferents also measure degree of stretch. These afferants feed into a spinal reflex. Sudden stretching fires off the muscle spindle, and causes a reflex muscle contraction. This mechanism is invoked when tendon reflexes are elicited.

Golgi bodies are found at the junction of tendon and muscle, and in ligaments. They appear to measure tension (see Fig. 2.9B).

Pacinian corpuscles are present in periosteum, interosseus membrane, in the deeper layers of joint capsules, and subcutaneously (see Fig. 2.9C). The receptor is made up of multiple concentric lamellae and contains fluid under pressure. The nerve ending responds to changes in turgor produced by vibration or grosser mechanical disturbance.

Ruffini organs are small encapsulated structures found in joint capsules which respond to mechanical stresses produced by movement (see Fig. 2.9D).

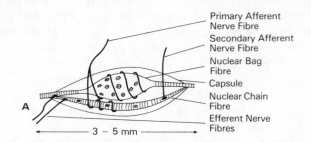

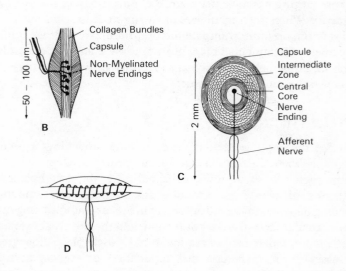

Fig. 2.9. Proprioceptive end-organs. A Muscle spindle. B. Golgi body. C. Pacinian corpuscle. D. Ruffni organ.

Finally there are free nerve endings inside joints situated in the capsule, fat pads and synovium which are stimulated by excessive movement and pressure, causing pain.

These end organs provide information at the conscious level about position and movement, and at the subconscious level elicit spinal reflexes which alter muscle action to control posture and prevent excessive deformation of joints and tissues. It is an exceedingly important system, and its failure results in loss of control of posture and complex movements.

The end organs cease functioning in the presence of inflammation, or prolonged immobilisation of a joint, and this loss of afferent input results in failure of postural reflexes, so that the joint gives way, a condition known as functional instability. It is particularly troublesome when joints of the lower limbs are involved, because posture has to be maintained continuously against the force of gravity. When treating injuries involving structures around a joint, it is very important to stimulate the proprioceptive endings from an early stage of treatment. This appears to prevent atrophy, certainly of some endings, and probably also recruits resting proprioceptive organs in the surrounding tissues.

EFFECTS OF INJURY

Whether the injury is due to a blow, twisting, stretching or friction, the immediate effect is damage to the structural elements of the tissue, such as muscle fibres, collagen or elastin, accompanied by rupturing of capillaries, arterioles and venules. The amount of bleeding depends on the vascularity of the tissue, muscle being much more vascular than ligament or tendon, and therefore liable to bleed much more. Other factors are involved. Muscle blood flow greatly increases during excercise due to dilation of the capillary bed coupled with an increased perfusion pressure. Age has an effect, as intramuscular bleeding is much more profuse in people in the mid-thirties and over, so that a small tear caused by a sudden sprint may cause a large haemorrhage. In joints the capsule and synovium are not particularly vascular, so if there is significant haemorrhage into a joint, it is likely to be due either to an endochondral fracture or to rupture of an intra-articular vascular structure. It is important to minimise bleeding into tissues as blood acts as an irritant, and will increase the amount of inflammation; also the cellular elements and fibrin of extravasated blood have to be removed before resolution can occur, and the greater the amount of bleeding, the longer this will take.

Acute inflammation

Damage to cells, tissues and blood vessels however caused, initiates the acute inflammatory reaction (Fig. 2.10). A transient constriction of arterioles is followed by vasodilation of arterioles and venules, opening up the capillary bed and causing widespread hyperaemia.

This phase may last from 10 minutes to several hours, depending on the volume of tissue damaged. The blood flow in the area may increase as much as ten-fold. Next the capillary bed becomes permeable to fluid and large molecules, because gaps are formed by retraction of the endothelial cells, and by changes in the basement membrane. The vasodilation, and loss of fluid into the tissue, results in the formation of a protein-rich inflammatory exudate. At the same

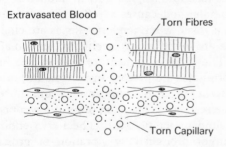

Fig. 2.10. Damaged tissue and capillaries.

12

time, there is a slowing of blood flow and leucocytes pavement around the periphery of the lumen. They then actively migrate through the vessel walls and tissues under chemotactic stimuli emanating from the region of tissue damage (see Fig. 2.11). At the end of this phase, which may last 24–48 hours, the extravascular spaces are distended with fluid, fibrin and cells arising from the acute inflammatory reaction. The vessels damaged in the original injury will have been sealed by platelet and fibrin plugs, but the extravasated blood will still be present in the tissues. The lymphocyte bed will also be dilated by tissue turgor and will be draining some of the extravascular fluid away. Clinically, the cardinal signs of inflammation will be present — heat, swelling, redness, pain and loss of function. The heat, swelling and redness are due to vascular changes and the presence of inflammatory exudate, the pain is due to increased tissue tension, and the presence of pharmacologically active substances stimulating pain nerve endings. The loss of function is partly due to a neurological reflex, and also to the swelling and tissue tension mechanically impeding movement.

This complex sequence of events making up the acute inflammatory reaction has evolved because although at first sight deleterious, it has survival value. It localises and dilutes any harmful substances. It mobilises phagocytic cells to the site of the damage, which then engulf debris, aided by the fibrin network in the intercellular spaces. It increases the local blood supply so that oxygen and nutrients are

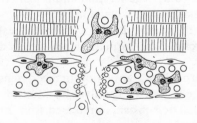

Fig. 2.11. Pavementing and emigration of leucocytes.

abundantly present, so facilitating subsequent processes of resolution and repair.

Acute inflammation is controlled and orchestrated by a host of chemical mediators (see Fig. 2.12). Histamine is released immediately from mast cells, eosinophils, basophils and platelets in the damaged capillaries, and causes transient local dilation and increased vascular permeability, lasting 10–15 minutes at the most. The initial damage allows the pro-enzyme of Hageman factor (factor XII) in the blood to be activated by exposure to basement membrane and extravascular collagen. It activates the kinin system so that kallikrein releases bradykinin from its kininogen precursor. Bradykinin is a potent promoter of vascular permeability and it also stimulates prostaglandin release from the endothelium. Hageman factor also activates the complement system, some of the products being of great importance in the inflammatory reaction, particularly C5a and C3a. These both increase vascular permeability, and are chemotactic. There is also a complex of factors C5, 6, 7 which is probably chemotactic. Finally, Hageman factor activates the coagulation and fibrinolytic systems. The latter involves plasmin, which in addition increases vascular permeability.

Arachidonic acid derivatives of various types are formed in most damaged tissues, and in platelets and leucocytes. Some of the prostaglandins (E1 and E2) are important in maintaining vasodilation and permeability in the later stages of the inflammatory reaction, and they also produce pain and fever. Other prostaglandins have effects on leucocyte adhesion and platelet aggregation. The leucotrienes are arachidonic acid derivatives produced by white cells and lymphocytes. Some are vasoactive and chemotactic.

To summarise, initial vasodilation is caused by histamine and maintained by prostaglandins (especially PGE2) and the complement components C3a and C5a. The increased vascular permeability is initiated by histamine and maintained by kinins, leucotrienes and probably prostaglandins. The emigration of leucocytes is stimulated by C5a and leucotrienes. Hageman factor is

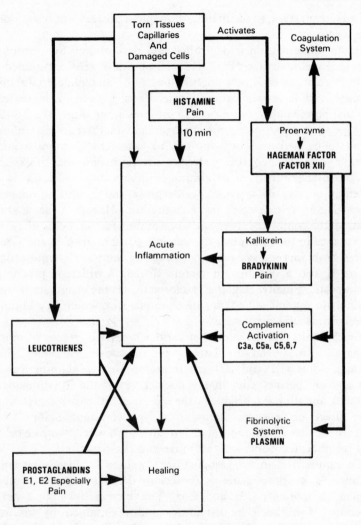

Fig. 2.12. Pharmacologically active mediators affecting healing processes.

of great importance in triggering and maintaining the changes. This is a much simplified account of a complex series of interactions which can augment and diminish the reactions so that the acute inflammatory process is very carefully controlled.

HEALING

Resolution

After 24–48 hours, the acute inflammatory process has localised the damage, and mobilised phagocytic cells into the area. Polymorphs and monocytes migrate from the capillary bed, and histocytes from surrounding connective tissue. The fibrin meshwork in the exudate provides a framework which enhances phagocytosis as these cells engulf cellular and other debris, and eventually the fibrin mesh itself. Fibronectin derived from plasma is also present, and enhances the activity of macrophages. As the cells clear the area, the fluid exudate is reabsorbed into capillaries and lymphocytes. If there has been little structural damage, the stage of resolution will result in a return to near normal.

Regeneration and repair

When tissue has been damaged, however, resolution leaves a gap which has to be filled by regeneration and repair. Bone regenerates well by callus formation, but skeletal muscle has little or no capacity for regeneration in mammals. In this case, healing is by scar formation or fibrosis. Scar formation also heals defects in other connective tissues.

Scar tissue is formed by granulation tissue; a dense population of fibroblasts nourished by a rich capillary bed. During the second day post injury chemotactic substances released from macrophages and platelets cause fibroblasts lying dormant in connective tissue to migrate into the area and become active. A local increase in hyaluronic acid draws in water, increases the amount of intercellular matrix and facilitates cell migration. An insoluble form of fibronectin is present in granulation tissue. It enhances cell adhesion and migration and is specifically chemotactic for fibroblasts. In addition, with fibrin it forms a temporary scaffold.

On the third day, capillary sprouts develop from surrounding blood vessels, grow into the area, ramify and join up, and canalise to form a capillary network (see Fig. 2.13). Initially they have no basement membrane, and consist of unsupported endothelial cells. At this stage, the capillary bed is very fragile and easily torn, and is liable to bleed. It is also permeable, and polymorphs, red cells and protein-rich fluid escape freely. After a few days, a basement membrane develops, and some of the vessels differentiate into arterioles and venules with muscular walls.

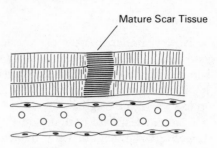

Fig. 2.14. Mature scar tissue.

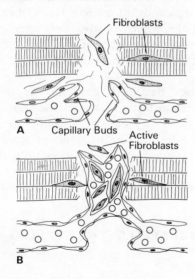

Fig. 2.13. A. Early formation of granulation tissue. B. Granulation tissue.

The fibroblasts in the granulation tissue are very active and produce collagen fibres and proteoglycan ground substance. Metabolic activity is at its height at 7 days, and the defect in the tissues is rapidly filled. By 20 days the quantity of collagen present is virtually maximal. However, this highly vascular new scar tissue has little tensile strength, and will tear easily and bleed profusely. It is also richly innervated with sensory endings, and sensitive to pressure and tension.

Changes take place as scar tissue matures. By 7 days post injury, continuity of the tissues is restored but the tensile strength is virtually nil. It gradually increases over the next 120 days to a maximum of 80–95% of the original strength of the tissue. At first the fibroblasts produce type III collagen (reticulin) which has very thin weak fibres. In time, this is replaced by type I (see Fig. 2.14). Increased inter-molecular bonding occurs between the collagen fibrils, shortening the scar. In response to mechanical stresses, the alignment of the fibres is remodelled by lysis and resynthesis so that fibres are lined up parallel to the lines of force. If the tissue is immobolised this does not occur, and the collagen is laid down haphazardly in a criss-cross pattern. As the scar tissue contracts, this will result in a tight puckered scar. As it matures it loses its vascularity and sensitivity.

Healing of ligaments and tendons

Mature scar tissue is very similar in structure to these tissues, and healing gives a good result. A complete tear of a ligament or tendon requires immediate referral to an orthopaedic surgeon as suturing may be needed. It will take 4 months to heal, and will achieve a tensile strength of up to 95% of the original.

However, most ligament tears are partial, and the joint remains stable. Functional recovery is much quicker if treated with intensive physiotherapy. The scar tissue will still take 4 months to achieve maturity, but once the pain and swelling of the acute inflammatory reaction have subsided, the remaining undamaged part of the ligament can take some tension, and the muscles surrounding the joint can be strengthened to take some of the force off the damaged ligament. If necessary, light strapping or support may be used temporarily. This early mobilisation leads to good linear scar formation, prevents the reflex wasting of muscles around the joint, and prevents loss of proprioceptive responses. However, it must be done carefully, and under close supervision — if the scar tissue is stressed too much it will tear, and cause further bleeding and inflammation. Repeated episodes of this sort result in a chronic sprain with formation of excess fibrous tissue, which is lumpy and tender.

Healing of torn muscle

Mature scar tissue is not at all like muscle. Muscle is extensible and elastic, whereas scar tissue is inelastic and although it will stretch to some extent if subjected to repeated pulling, it will if immobilised tend to contract slowly as it matures. If a puckered scar is allowed to form in muscle, it will give repeated trouble. As the muscle stretches during exercise, it will pull on the scar, giving discomfort and a sensation of tightness which will impair performance. Worse, such a tight scar is liable to tear, causing bleeding and inflammation with more scar formation and disability — a chronic sprain.

This can be prevented by graded stretching and light exercise during healing, so that the scar is formed with its fibres parallel to the line of pull; regular repeated stretching will cause the collagen fibres to elongate and form a lax rather than a puckered scar. Scar tissue retains its capacity to contract for long periods if not indefinitely, so the patient must be taught to stretch and warm up properly before exercising.

Enthesopathy

This is a tear of muscle fibres directly off their insertion into periosteum, e.g. lateral epicondylitis of the elbow (tennis elbow) where the common extensor origin becomes partially detached from the lateral epicondyle of the humerus by repeated forced wrist extension. Medial epicondylitis (golfers' elbow) is caused by repeated forced flexion at the wrist, stressing the common flexor origin. Another example is the avulsion of the upper fibres of adductor magnus from the pubic ramus caused by forced abduction of the hip.

In all these cases, healing is slow and the condition tends to become chronic because forces on the muscle origin are considerable and there is no satisfactory way of offloading them while the scar matures. Therefore the new scar tissue tends to get stressed and bleed repeatedly. This leads to the formation of a knot of chronic inflammatory tissue which remains tender. In this type of injury, it is essential to ensure adequate rest for proper healing to occur.

FACTORS WHICH AFFECT THE HEALING PROCESS

Blood supply

If the injured area has a poor blood supply, healing is delayed. Measures to improve the local blood supply will enhance the supply of oxygen and nutrients to the actively metabolising granulation tissue and speed up the formation of adequate scar tissue. Many of the physiotherapy modalities do this, e.g. ice treatment, short-wave diathermy, ultrasound (see Chapter 3).

Infection

Bacteria delay healing, and all infected wounds should be treated with appropriate systemic antibiotics.

Nutritional deficiencies

Under experimental conditions, deficiencies of vitamin C, the sulphur-containing amino acids and zinc all interfere with collagen synthesis. The fibres formed are atypical and weak, and in addition the capillaries in the granulation tissue do not develop a basement membrane, and so bleed very readily.

Such nutritional deficiencies are unlikely to occur in patients attending a Sports Injury Clinic. Unless there is a deficiency to correct, administration of vitamin C, zinc or methionine has no effect on healing.

Glucocorticosteroids

Large doses of these hormones suppress repair. They reduce the activity of polymorphs and macrophages in the inflammatory reaction, and have a suppressive effect on the formation of granulation tissue because they inhibit fibroblast migration and proliferation, and the formation of new capillaries. They not only delay scar formation, but the scar that is formed is weak and substandard. There is therefore no place for corticosteroid hormones in the treatment of acute tears in muscle, ligaments and tendons.

There are a few special circumstances where they are helpful in the management of acute soft tissue injuries. They may be used by local injection to suppress acute inflammation where this is causing pain and impaired function; e.g. acute tenosynovitis and peri-tendinitis, bursitis and synovitis, provided it is certain no infection is present. Injections of corticosteroids may also be used to suppress chronic inflammatory tissue, as in chronic tennis elbow, where a palpable knot of tender scar tissue is present. Many of these conditions will settle with rest and appropriate physiotherapy — wherever possible these measures should be tried first, and the corticosteroid only used if they fail.

Prostaglandin synthetase inhibitors

After the first 24–48 hours, much of the pain from a soft tissue injury appears to be due to local release of prostaglandins, and these also contribute to local oedema and vasodilation. Giving prostaglandin synthetase inhibitors (non-steroidal anti-inflammatory drugs or NSAIDs) appears to ease pain and swelling without slowing or impeding healing. As they reduce pain, they tend to enable the patient to comply with the mobilising treatment. These drugs are therefore very useful in the treatment of soft tissue injuries, and a course of 7–10 days is usually adequate.

Exercise

Local exercise to the affected part strengthens agonist muscles, which in turn takes load off the injured structures. It ensures the scar gets stretched regularly during healing, so that it forms parallel to the direction of pull and is supple. It maintains joint mobility and muscle balance and prevents loss of proprioceptive reflexes. These factors all contribute to an early return to full function.

Such exercise has to be given under careful supervision, so that the damaged area is not stressed too much or too soon.

General exercise maintains the individual's state of cardiovascular and respiratory fitness. This general fitness declines very rapidly if regular exercise is reduced for even a few days. It is particularly noticeable in trained athletes, and in addition to its measurable physical effects, leads to a feeling of depression and apathy. Therefore wherever possible some alternative form of exercise should be encouraged whilst the athlete is unable to train normally. Swimming or cycling (on the road or on an exercise cycle) are often possible with lower limb or trunk injuries.

The physiotherapist will prescribe and supervise local exercises, and once satisfied the patient is adequately fit, will allow him to return to training. It is very important that before playing or competing, the athlete returns to the training programme and gets fully fit.

QUEEN E... CANCELLED ...RY,
CENTRAL BIRMINGHAM HEALTH DISTRI... PHYSIOTH...

Physiotherapy is the most important treatment for the majority of soft tissue injuries. If started early and used intensively, it speeds up the resolution of damage, prevents the development of chronic problems and returns the individual to full activity more quickly. The presence of a capable chartered physiotherapist is essential for any Sports Injury Clinic. Physiotherapy embraces a wide range of techniques and modalities, and the following is a brief survey of these.

PHYSICAL TECHNIQUES

MASSAGE

Effective massage is labour intensive. It will increase the blood flow locally, disperse oedema fluid, break down fibrinous adhesions, and reduce local muscle spasm. It is particularly useful for relieving muscle stiffness and soreness. It can be used before exercise to increase muscle blood flow and reduce muscle tension, and there are some top performers in sport and entertainment who regard a full body massage as essential before they perform. However, this is something of a luxury, and beyond the reach of most athletes. It is also not as effective as the recommended stretching and warm-up routine which, in addition to getting muscles supple, also gets the body as a whole into a state of preparedness.

FRICTIONS

This is a form of hard localised rubbing done either with the fingers or with a vibrating applicator. When applied over areas of chronic scar tissue, it breaks down cross adhesions, stretches the scar and improves the blood supply. Over a period of time, it will improve the orientation of collagen fibres and make the scar more linear and extensible. Coupled with stretching, it is one of the best treatments for chronic scar tissue in muscles or ligaments. Unfortunately it is quite painful initially. Some practitioners also use it on acute injuries, and claim it prevents adhesions forming.

Embrocations and liniments may be used with massage or frictions. They lubricate the skin and as they contain rubefacients they produce a comfortable glow in the skin. However, any real effect in the deeper tissues is due to the mechanical effect of the rubbing.

MOBILISATION AND MANIPULATION

These specialised techniques are invaluable for correcting certain mechanical joint problems. They may be used to correct an acute displacement — e.g. in the apophyseal joints of the spine, or a prolapsed intervertebral disc. Another use is to break down adhesions in a joint which have developed following a haemarthrosis due to trauma or surgery. It should only be done by a trained person, and after an X-ray has excluded any unexpected abnormalities such as a fracture or a tumour.

STRETCHING

Regular stretching is very important during the healing of a muscle tear, as it stimulates correct orientation of the collagen fibres and counteracts the natural tendency of maturing fibrous tissue to shorten and pucker. The aim is to have a soft, elongated and flexible scar orientated parallel to the direction of pull of the muscle. If the muscle is rested and not stretched, the collagen tends to be laid down criss-cross, and then contracts into a bunched-up knot, very likely to tear when the muscle is stretched, and to become a chronic problem. The patient can be taught a stretching regime which should be practised in the warm-up before exercise even after full recovery, as scar tissue remains likely to contract long after it is formed.

EXERCISES

The majority of soft tissue injuries benefit from exercise. Movement appears to enhance sound scar formation in muscles, tendons and ligaments, and to improve the tensile strength of the mature scar. This is possibly because it stimulates the formation of cross-linking between collagen fibres. It also means that the fibroblasts lay down collagen fibres parallel to the forces acting on the tissue, resulting in a linear scar, which will eventually, if stretched regularly, form a supple, elongated scar.

In the early stages, fresh scar tissue is highly vascular, and has no tensile strength, so that exercise must be carefully supervised and graded.

Exercise is also used to prevent the wasting which otherwise occurs in the agonists and antagonists around an injury, and strengthening these muscles will offload the damaged region. As recovery continues, it is important to maintain muscle balance around a joint and also between the two sides of the body.

Isometric exercises may be used initially — by tensing the muscle without moving a joint, they stimulate muscle fibres and apply gentle but not undue stress to scar tissue. As recovery proceeds, graded active exercises are introduced against increasing resistance. Final strengthening can be done using isokinetic exercise on a suitable machine. Isokinetic exercise involves the muscle working against a constant force throughout the full range of the joint. This is believed to produce maximum strength but requires specially geared apparatus to supply the uniform resistance.

Once mobile, a combination of exercise and balancing is used to stimulate the proprioceptive system and re-educate reflex postural control. Graded exercises on the rocking and spherical-based wobbleboards are excellent. They can be combined with daily exercises running circles and curves, or bending through a line of markers, progressively increasing the tightness of the curves. These provide excellent stimulation of proprioceptors in ankles, knees, hips and lower spine. This is very important for getting full functional recovery.

General exercise is also important and whenever possible the injured athlete should be recommended some form of aerobic exercise whilst off customary training and sport. Swimming and cycling are possible with many lower limb injuries; walking or running with upper limb injuries. This prevents the level of cardio-respiratory fitness declining too far, and helps maintain a sense of well-being and purpose.

STRAPPING AND SUPPORT

Some coaches, physiotherapists and doctors use strapping a great deal, employing routine strapping of joints which are healthy, but known to be at risk for the sport, e.g. ankles in netball. In the opinion of the author, this is a mistake — the strapping immobilises the joint, weakening the agonist and antagonist muscles, and puts more strain on neighbouring joints. It also inactivates the normal proprioceptive input from the joint, and this impairs the normal pattern of body movements. Both of these factors may lead to injury — not of the strapped joint, it is true, but elsewhere.

Other people use heavy strapping on recently injured joints to allow them to compete. The same drawbacks apply, and if the strapping is necessary to allow play, then that person is not ready to return to competition.

In general, the best protection for a joint is a set of strong and balanced muscles, with an intact postural feedback response stimulated by the proprioceptive end organs in and around the joint. Sometimes a light strapping is useful; e.g. T-strapping an ankle or wearing a Tubigrip, because the skin contact stimulates additional mechanoreceptors in the skin, reinforcing the postural reflexes. This type of support does not embarrass movement.

THERMAL TECHNIQUES

HEAT

This is a traditional treatment for stiff and painful joints and muscles. Its actions are to produce vasodilation, muscle relaxation, relief of pain and sedation. The vasodilation is a direct effect of heating tissues, but since heat is poorly conducted, the effect is only very superficial. Pain relief is due to counter-irritation in most cases. (An exception to this is the inactivation of some venoms by heat. The painful sting inflicted by the spines on the back of a stingray can be alleviated by plunging the foot in water as hot as can be borne — the heat denatures the protein of the venom, and removes its pain-producing effect.)

Heat can be applied in various ways, e.g. immersion in hot water, paraffin wax baths, hot towels, electrically heated pads, and infra-red lamps. An infra-red laser has recently been developed, and is under evaluation. The effect of the heat is always the same, so the method most easily available and convenient for the part of the body should be used.

ICE OR COLD THERAPY

Although it sounds unappealing, this is a more effective way of producing deep vasodilation than heat. It also has a pain-relieving effect, and reduces muscle spasm. When skin is chilled, there is initially local vasoconstriction, but after 5–10 minutes the blood flow through superficial and deep tissues increases and then oscillates. This 'hunting' effect appears to promote resorption of exudate and the increased blood flow increases the temperature and improves tissue nutrition. This effect extends quite deeply into the subcutaneous tissues including muscle — much deeper than that produced by local heat.

Ice can be applied for short periods at a time to produce vasoconstriction and reduce bleeding in a fresh injury. It should not be left on for long periods when used for first aid, as this will cause vasodilation and increase tissue haemorrhage. An ice pack should be put on for about 5 minutes and then a compressive bandage applied, the part elevated and the victim rested (the RICE regime).

The most effective way to chill the skin is to use melting ice at 0°C. The latent heat of fusion is 336 J/g, so each gram of ice extracts 491 J as it is warmed to 37°C, whereas water at 0°C would only extract 155 J over the same range: i.e. melting ice is just over three times more chilling.

Another reason for using melting ice is that it is no colder than 0°C, and not liable to cause skin damage from ice burns. Freezer packs (or packets of frozen peas!) may be very cold and cause burns, and since they cool less efficiently than wet ice, they are not really to be recommended, even though they are convenient. A very few people develop cold urticaria when the skin is chilled — this will subside spontaneously, but further ice treatment should be avoided.

Ice can be applied as a pack or an iced towel. The skin should first be oiled to prevent burning, and a plastic sheet should be put underneath to prevent a flood. Some regions, e.g. foot, hand or elbow, can be immersed in a bowl containing a slurry of ice and water. A localised area, e.g. a bruise on the forehead, can be rubbed with an ice cube. The cold sprays used to such dramatic effect by coaches on the pitch produce a transient chilling too brief to cause any vascular effects — the stimulus may be a counter-irritant, and there is a big placebo effect.

After the first 24 hours, when there is no danger of further bleeding, ice should be used for about 10 minutes to produce vasodilation. This causes considerable local discomfort at first, and it has been known for people to faint — the patient should therefore be reclining and supervised. When the ice is removed, the skin is bright red, due to hyperaemia. Pain is reduced, and muscle spasm relaxed, making this a good time to perform some exercises.

Ice treatment is simple to administer and patients can do it at home, several times a day, if necessary. It is also an excellent first aid measure.

ELECTRICAL TECHNIQUES

There is now available a wide range of machines using mains electricity or battery power, recommended (at any rate by their manufacturers) in the management of soft tissue injuries. Some have become part of the standard armamentarium of physiotherapy departments, although there have been relatively few controlled trials of their effectiveness. Some modalities produce obvious effects on the tissues, and their action is well-understood. Others appear to help, but it is less certain by what means. There is potentially a strong placebo effect from any complicated piece of apparatus.

The following is a brief account of some of these modalities — it will inevitably be out of date before long.

SHORT-WAVE DIATHERMY

This is a well-tried method of producing heating in deep tissues. A high frequency alternating current is used to generate electromagnetic waves in the tissue, and these agitate the molecules in cells and extracellular fluid producing direct heating. By convention a current of 27.12 MHz is used for medical purposes, avoiding interfering with radio, TV and short-wave radios. There are various types of machines used for short-wave therapy — by various means they induce an electromagnetic current in the tissues between electrodes placed close to the skin in such a way as to heat the required area.

The current passes through all tissues so it is a good way of affecting lesions too deep for ice therapy, or where intervening bone would reflect ultrasound waves (see below). The electrical impedance of tissues varies, e.g. high in fat, low in muscle, and tissues respond differently to parallel and transverse electrical fields. These facts can be used to cause differential heating of tissues. Short-wave diathermy should only be administered by a trained person, as there is danger of producing burns or electric shock. It should not be used where there is any form of metal implant, in tissues treated by radiotherapy or near a tumour.

ULTRASOUND

This is a very useful treatment for acute and chronic soft tissue injuries. When ultrasound energy is absorbed by the tissues, heat is released, causing local heat and an increase in blood flow secondary to this. In addition, it appears to have a direct analgesic effect on nerve endings which persists a short while after cessation of treatment. It may have direct stimulating effects on certain cells, e.g. fibroblasts, and appears to influence the alignment of collagen. The vibration of macromolecules in tissue fluids may directly enhance absorption of oedema fluid into the blood vessels and lymphatics. This effect is especially useful in acute inflammation.

The ultrasonic waves are usually 1 or 3 MHz. They are generated by electrically stimulating a piezo-electric crystal in the head of the machine. The crystal vibrates and when held against the skin, the ultrasound waves are transmitted to the tissues. The beam is reflected off bony surfaces and therefore is not useful for treating tissue behind bone — not only do the waves not reach the target region but the reflected beam may interact with the incident beam and set up a standing wave causing excessive local heating.

Ultrasound may be used in continuous or pulsed form. The continuous mode produces maximal local heating. In the pulsed mode, the intervals between pulses allow some of the heat to be dispersed by conduction through diffusion and perfusion by blood, and therefore larger doses can be given.

Ultrasound can be applied by moving the crystal-containing head over the skin, keeping it at right angles to the surface, so that the waves pass directly into the tissues. A coupling gel is used because air does not transmit the waves. Water transmits the ultrasound well, so it can also be administered by immersing both body part, e.g. foot or hand, and the treatment head in a container of water, or by applying the head of the instrument to a water-filled bag lying on the skin.

Continuous exposure of a tissue may produce local burns, so the head should be moved throughout treatment. Ultrasound should not be used in the presence of infection or tumour, or on skin which has been irradiated.

FARADISM

Faradism is sometimes useful in a Sports Injury Clinic, to re-educate the patient in the use of a particular muscle. It is no substitute for active exercise, although it will produce some increase in muscle bulk, and should be used only in the early stages of rehabilitation. It is, however, invaluable in teaching conscious control over muscles, e.g. the intrinsic muscles of the feet, or the vastus medialis in the thigh. An interrupted direct electric current is conducted through tissues. It causes depolarisation of nerves, mimicking spontaneous nerve impulses. It stimulates motor nerves, causing contraction, and sensory nerves, producing quite a pleasant paraesthetic sensation. To avoid muscle fatigue, the current is surged, allowing intermittent

relaxation. A frequency of 50–100 Hz is used in pulses of 0.1–1 milliseconds.

The faradic current can be transmitted to the body either through electrodes strapped to the skin over the muscle, or when treating the tarsal interossei it is convenient to use a water bath. The surges of current produce regular contractions, and the patient should be encouraged to contract the muscle voluntarily at the same time. It usually only takes two or three sessions before the patient has sufficient voluntary control to embark on active exercises.

A variant on the use of faradism is functional electrical stimulation. The patient performs a maximal contraction and then the current is switched on and produces a further contraction, demonstrating to the patient that a greater effort is possible.

INTERFERENTIAL TREATMENT

This apparatus produces a low frequency electromagnetic field (see below) of the order of 100 Hz. Due to high skin impedance, it is difficult to get adequate penetration by low frequency currents. To overcome this, these machines utilise two crossing medium frequency currents, and where they interfere with each other, a beat frequency develops at a lower frequency. Four electrodes are placed on the skin, and positioned so that the currents intersect in the injured region. One of the currents can be varied, thus altering the frequency of the interference field.

The two main effects appear to be pain relief and absorption of oedema fluid. Relief of pain is at any rate partly due to the low frequency electro-magnetic field having a direct effect on sensory nerves. Motor stimulation also occurs and is said to affect involuntary as well as skeletal muscle. Intermittent stimulation of arteriolar muscle producing a pulsing effect may be what causes the absorption of oedema. However, the nature and efficacy of the effects of interferential treatment have yet to be established experimentally.

Unlike faradism, the patient is unable to contract voluntarily with the contractions.

PULSED ELECTROMAGNETIC ENERGY

As already described, short-wave diathermy produces direct heating of tissues by electromagnetic waves, and this technique has been in use for decades. Whilst the predominant effects are due to heating, it has been suspected for some time that there might be other effects due to the electromagnetic field. With the development of machines which emit pulsed electromagnetic energy, it has become possible to separate these two effects. Short pulses of energy are interspersed with rest periods in a ratio in the region of 1 on, to 35–40 off, repeated from 100–800 pulses per second. The heat generated during the brief on period is dispersed during the off period, and there is no significant heating effect. The high frequency energy consists of electrical and magnetic fields. The apparatus delivering it may be made so that one or the other predominates, or both may be emitted simultaneously. This is probably of limited significance as the tissues are not inert, and in the presence of a magnetic field, an electric field is generated and vice versa, so that an isolated electric or magnetic effect is never achieved.

It has become apparent that electromagnetic energy does have direct effects on cells, but their precise nature is as yet unclear. There may be separate effects on the processes of resolution and repair. Normal cells have an electric potential across the cell membrane (the membrane potential), which is of the order of -70mV. This is maintained by the balance of ions across the membrane. Under normal conditions, there is a higher concentration of potassium ions inside the cell, and of sodium ions outside. Specific ion channels in the membrane allow ions to pass through the membrane according to concentration gradients. The sodium ion concentration inside the cell is kept low by the sodium pump, which moves sodium ions against the concentration gradient.

Cells that are damaged have a membrane potential reduced to around -40mV. It is likely that the sodium pump fails as the concentration of sodium ions rises inside the cell. When these changes become irreversible, the cell dies, but a 'sick' cell may recover. It is postulated that the pulsed electromagnetic field may in some way restore the membrane potential and the function of the sodium pump, or possibly make the sodium pump work at above normal rate, so that the cell returns to normal. This would perhaps rescue otherwise doomed cells, and would speed resolution of inflammation. The effect on sick cells seems to be like a switch, in that a short exposure appears to be sufficient.

There is also evidence that there is a direct effect on the function of fibroblasts and osteoblasts. Collagen appears to be laid down more rapidly and the fibres are better orientated, resulting in good quality scar tissue. Osteoblasts may be stimulated and osteogenesis induced in fractures that have previously failed to unite. These effects influence repair and require continuous or repetitive exposure to a pulsed electromagnetic field for full effect.

It should be emphasised that at the moment, much of this is speculative, and requires experimental verification.

Other effects noted are dispersion of oedema and relief of pain. Machines are available to produce high or low frequency pulsed electromagnetic fields.

High frequency pulsed electromagnetic energy: This modality of treatment involves frequencies up to 600 pulses and is delivered through a single head. The patient feels nothing as there is no heating, and at these frequencies no motor or sensory stimulation occurs. There are a variety of machines on the market, some of which emit both electric and magnetic fields, whilst others can be adjusted to deliver only electric or only magnetic fields. The effects are said to be quicker resolution of inflammation and enhancement of healing. Pain relief may be due to the suppression of inflammation and removal of the nociceptive substances associated with it.

It should not be used on people with cardiac pacemakers, or pregnant women (neither group being seen much in a Sports Injury Clinic!).

Low frequency pulsed electromagnetic fields: These are for continuous treatment, and are being evaluated in the treatment of chronic soft-tissue inflammation and non-healing fractures. The battery-powered apparatus is encased in a mould shaped to the body part under treatment, and sets up a pulsed low frequency electromagnetic field. It is used for weeks or months at a time.

THE SPORTS INJURY TREATMENT GYM

Some of the machines discussed above are very expensive, and as their value is not yet proven, they are by no means essential to a clinic of limited means.

Basic requirements would be an ice machine, ultrasound, short-wave diathermy, an infra-red lamp, a good range of sand-bags and weights, rocking and spherical-based wobbleboards, a balance bench and some plastic footballs and skittles. Other items can be added as funds allow.

The design of the treatment area should be open plan, with plinths along the side, and one or two curtainable areas to allow privacy where necessary.

This arrangement means the physiotherapist can supervise a number of simultaneous activities, which is essential, as the clinics tend to be busy, many patients having daily treatment for 1–2 weeks.

A typical treatment session e.g. for someone with a sprained ankle, would be first an ice pack with the affected ankle elevated, then application of ultrasound, followed by graded exercises. These can be done in groups, and in the later stages of rehabilitation; games on the wobbleboard and contests involving hopping on and off the bench, or dribbling a ball through a line of skittles, add a competitive element. The aim is to get each individual fit enough to go back to regular training before competing again. Group activities are good for morale, and compliance is usually excellent in these highly motivated people.

The Sports Injury Clinic should have an educative role in addition to diagnosis and treatment. During the course of treatment, the physiotherapist and doctor should explore the possible reasons underlying the injury, e.g. inadequate training, insufficient warm-up, worn or unsuitable apparatus, poor technique, conditions of pitch, going on too long after fatigued, etc. Of course, some injuries, especially in contact sports, are due to external forces, and totally unpreventable by the individual. The nature of the injury, and rationale of treatment should be explained, suitable stretching and warm-up techniques taught, and measures to avoid its recurrence discussed. The principles of first aid and self-treatment, e.g. with ice, are also taught. This can all be done quite informally during the patient's visits. It is hoped by heightening self-awareness and knowledge of body mechanics, each athlete will be motivated to maintain proper fitness and help avoid further injuries. This counselling and the instruction on adequate first aid also tends to get disseminated through the club or team.

Characteristic Effects and Treatment
of Trauma in Tissues

The different reactions of tissues influence their response to trauma, and must be considered when choosing appropriate treatment. These general characteristics of tissues are discussed here, and in the section on diagnosis (p. 51), the local features of specific injuries are mentioned under the relevant body parts.

SKIN

Cuts and grazes

Small cuts and grazes are common in contact sports. Extensive grazing may occur from falling on the modern all-weather surfaces. The wound should be cleaned and any gravel or mud removed. Iodine or mercurochrome should be applied. Dry dressings may be used, but where possible it is better left undressed.

Deep cuts should be sutured or pulled together with butterfly sutures or Steristrips. Infected wounds should be cultured and treated with appropriate systemic antibiotic.

Anyone with a deep or extensive wound should have a booster tetanus toxoid injection.

Blisters

Friction separates the superficial layer of skin and an outpouring of fluid results in a tense, distended lesion. Blisters occur on feet as a result of friction with footwear, or on hands from gripping racquets, oars etc. They are common, painful and can wreck performance. Prevention is the best treatment. Footwear should be comfortable and fit properly, the uppers should be made of a breathing material like leather or canvas, and not plastic. Thick socks with a looped towel-like finish are best, and should be wool or cotton. They should either have no seams, or the seams should be placed away from pressure areas. Areas where friction is anticipated can be protected with moleskin. Some people advocate hardening the skin with surgical spirit rubs, and using talcum powder to lubricate the skin. It is important to keep skin and socks or gloves fresh and clean.

Once blisters have formed, it is probably best to puncture them with a sterile needle, drain the fluid out, and then wear a plaster dressing of the breathing type. An alternative is to strip the roof off the blister and apply zinc oxide tape directly to the raw base.

Corns and calluses

In response to local long-standing friction or pressure, excess keratin is produced locally, forming yellowish hard areas, which protect the skin. However, if the layer of keratin becomes very thick and hard, pressure on it distorts the underlying dermis, causing pain.

On the feet, calluses and corns are usually the result of badly fitting footwear. The shoe may be a bad shape, e.g. shoes with a narrow toe, compress and flex the toes, and corns occur under the metatarsal heads, over the base of the hallux and on the dorsum of the flexed toes. Alternatively, the foot may be misshapen, so that undue loading occurs at pressure spots, e.g. hallux valgus, or collapsed arches due to weak intrinsic foot muscles.

On the hands, calluses form where the grip presses on oars or racquets, and is beneficial unless it gets too thick, when it may crack and the skin underneath become infected.

Calluses can be kept to a reasonable thickness by regular rubbing with pumice after soaking in warm water — this is most easily done in the bath.

Skin infections

Contagious skin infections can be transmitted between athletes by contact during sport, particularly where communal bathing occurs, or by sharing clothing or gear, e.g. herpes simplex, staphylococcal impetigo, dermatophyte infections such as ringworm and athletes' foot. The infection should be treated with the appropriate agent and the athlete excluded from close contact with others until no longer infectious.

SUBCUTANEOUS TISSUE

Bruises

Local knocks cause subcutaneous haematomas, which are usually small and recover over a period of days, during which the extravasated blood changes from red to bluish purple, to green, to yellow. In most regions the surrounding tissues are lax enough to accommodate the swelling, and no treatment is needed. Where subcutaneous tissue is tight, the swelling causes pressure and pain, e.g. skin, fingers, nose and ears, and in this case the application of an ice-pack as first-aid reduces the swelling, and regular treatment with ice thereafter speeds resolution.

MUSCLE

Muscle is a vascular tissue and the vascularity increases on exercising, so haemorrhage is a prominent feature of muscle injuries.

Direct blows

A direct blow to muscle will cause intramuscular haemorrhage. This is particularly liable to occur in the bulky muscles of the thigh, where

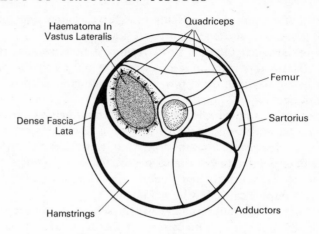

Fig. 4.1. Mid-thigh section showing effect of intramuscular haematoma.

kneeing or kicking to the vastus lateralis can cause massive bleeding of more than 0.5 litre (see Fig. 4.1). As the muscle is enclosed by inelastic fascia, expansion is limited, and there is a rise in intramuscular tension which restricts movement of the muscle. Rarely the pressure rises above arterial pressure, causing ischaemia, and then emergency surgery is required to relieve tension and prevent gangrene.

Usually the haemorrhage extravasates between the muscle fibres and then clots. The presence of blood elicits an acute inflammatory reaction which causes more swelling and tension, and pain may be severe in the first 2–3 days. Pyrogens and other products of decaying red cells from a big haemorrhage cause systemic malaise and fever, and a moderate leucocytosis.

On examination, there may be marks or abrasions at the point of impact. There is a tense, tender swelling several inches across, the muscle can only contract partially, if at all, and the space-occupying nature of the haemorrhage limits muscle relaxation and impairs passive movement at the joint or joints it acts on.

The extravasated blood is slowly removed by phagocytosis, the acute inflammatory reaction resolves, and the muscle tear heals, but full recovery may take up to 6 weeks, depending on the size of the haemorrhage.

It is not usually possible to aspirate blood in the acute stage, as it is dispersed between muscle fibres and of a jelly-like consistency. Indeed, it is unwise to attempt aspiration, as the needle-track may allow bacterial infection of the vulnerable clot. (Sometimes after a week to 10 days, a loculated fluctuant swelling of encysted fluid develops, and this can safely be aspirated.)

Treatment consists of rest and daily physiotherapy with ice packs, followed by ultrasound. This latter may disrupt remaining erythrocytes by sonication, and speed the dispersal. The patient may need to be on crutches and non-weight-bearing initially. Gentle passive movements and static exercises progress to non-weight-bearing active exercises, and gradual return to activity. Mobilisation should be slow: too rapid return to activity causes further intramuscular bleeds. In certain sites, e.g. the quadriceps and elbow muscles, this leads to intramuscular calcium deposition which may become organised into bone — myositis ossificans. With an intramuscular haematoma of the quadriceps the patient should not be allowed to weight-bear until knee flexion is at least 90°.

Muscle tears

If a muscle is stretched suddenly or too far, some of the fibres will tear, and bleeding will occur in the muscle. Where a bunch of muscle fibres tear, it may produce a sensation of snapping or popping, or even of being struck from the outside. Fibres tearing under tension occasionally cause an audible crack. The bleeding into the muscle causes local irritation, resulting in a cramp or spasm.

In the common muscle pull or strain, only a small proportion of fibres is involved. Such injuries may occur soon after beginning activity, particularly if the individual has not stretched and warmed up adequately, and if the weather is cold. The other time they are likely to occur is late in the game or event when the athlete is tiring, and movements are less well co-ordinated.

Occasionally a muscle may rupture totally, e.g. rectus femoris may rupture in weight-lifters or footballers. Surgical repair may be undertaken immediately, but once the ends have retracted, is impossible.

Older individuals (35+) tend to bleed much more from torn muscles. A sudden sprint for the ball (or a bus) may cause a partial tear of hamstring or calf muscles, accompanied by profuse bleeding. The bulk of the haemorrhage is usually intramuscular (see above), though it will track eventually to the surface, and give spectacular bruising.

On examination, there may be swelling of the muscle. Visible bruising on the skin usually appears a few days after the injury, the blood having tracked to the surface. The influence of gravity usually causes it to appear below the original tear. There is localised tenderness over the injury. On palpation there may be some local resistance, due to muscle spasm or local haematoma, and after 10 or more days, a knot of scar tissue may be palpable. When the muscle contracts against resistance, pain is felt at the site of injury.

In the case of a total tear, there may be a palpable gap, with the bunched-up torn ends of muscle on either side. However, the gap may not be felt, because it is filled with blood and effusion. The clue then is that attempts at active contraction produce no movement.

If there is no local tenderness, and no pain on resisted movement, the problem is not in the muscle, and some other cause for the symptoms must be sought. For instance, pain in the back of the thigh may be self-diagnosed by the athlete as a hamstring tear, when it is in fact referred pain in the S1 dermatome from a low back problem.

Treatment in the form of physiotherapy should be early and intensive to ensure good recovery. Prompt first aid using the RICE regime (rest, ice, compression and elevation) will limit the amount of acute bleeding. Subsequently ice and ultrasound are used, followed by stretching and graded active exercises. The surrounding muscles are strengthened to reduce the load on the injured muscle. It is important that balance between agonists and antagonists is maintained. Return to normal activities is usually possible in 1–2 weeks, depending on the size of the tear.

When there is a sizeable intramuscular haemorrhage, mobilisation should be slow and the limb should be non-weight-bearing, if passive joint movement is limited. In the case of a hamstring tear, this means less than full knee extension, and in the case of a calf injury, dorsiflexion at the ankle of less than 90°.

In general, total rest is very bad for muscle injuries, as the muscle wastes and the scar contracts. Convalescence is then prolonged and the contracted scar is liable to tear when subsequently stressed. NSAIDs are helpful in the more extensive tears.

If a large proportion of muscle is torn, return to sport should be delayed for at least 3–4 weeks, as there is not sufficient healthy muscle to take the strain off the injured region. The newly-formed scar is very vascular for 3–4 weeks, and if stretched will tear easily, causing more haemorrhage and inflammation. After this has occurred 2–3 times, an area of chronic scar tissue forms, and gives pain and limitation of movement. This type of problem often besets sprinters. A typical story is that early in the athletic season, a hamstring strain occurs. The athlete, keen to get back to competition, races again after about 10 days, when the muscle is feeling better, but in fact the scar is barely formed, is highly vascular, and has no tensile strength. It tears and bleeds and the cycle is repeated, perhaps several times. When advice is eventually sought, there will be a palpable tender knot of chronic scar tissue in the muscle. Such an injury is very slow to recover, and may take weeks of treatment with frictions (which are painful), stretching and gradual strengthening to heal it. If the athlete had been prepared to be out of competition for 4 weeks after the initial injury, total recovery would have been much quicker.

After an injury, scar tissue retains its capacity to contract for long periods, if not indefinitely, so the athlete should be shown a stretching routine and cautioned to practise this routinely for at least 10 minutes before exercise.

Local injection of corticosteroids into torn muscle suppresses the inflammatory reaction, giving relief of pain for up to 24 hours. However, since corticosteroids impair scar formation, in the long run the effects are deleterious, and it is not good practice.

If an athlete is desperate to compete in some very special event, an injection of local anaesthetic into the tender area of muscle given just before the event will relieve pain just as effectively, with fewer harmful effects. Further tearing is a likely consequence, and except for 'once in a lifetime' events, it is best to keep an athlete away from competition until full fitness is restored.

TENDON INJURIES

Tendons are very strong, and do not rupture at all easily. If a strong traction force is applied to a healthy tendon, it is more likely to avulse the bony origin, or tear the musculo-tendinous junction than to tear the tendon itself.

Tendons have a poor blood supply and with increasing age, this becomes impaired, so that degenerative changes develop in the tendon, rendering it more likely to tear if stressed (see Fig. 4.2). This is particularly likely to occur at certain sites. For instance, the Achilles tendon receives its main blood supply from either end. The junction of the lower third and upper two-thirds of the tendon is the end of the run for both blood supplies, and with overuse and age this region becomes ischaemic. Degenerative changes inside the tendon cause a central cyst which results in potential weakness. Sometimes the cyst enlarges to cause visible distension and local soreness. In other cases, the first indication of degeneration may be a sudden partial or complete tear.

At the shoulder, the tendon of the supraspinatus muscle may catch

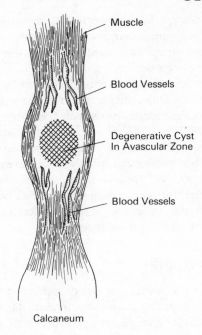

Fig. 4.2. Achilles tendon.

below the acromion. The friction causes degenerative changes, and in this site calcium salts frequently become deposited in the damaged tissue. Sometimes an attack of pain seems to be associated with extrusion of these calcium salts from the tendon. This is a common finding in middle-aged or elderly people. In racquet players, it occurs at an earlier age, as they often develop a postural droop on the shoulder of the racquet arm, so that the acromion impinges more on the supraspinatus tendon — the movements for overhead shots and service increase the friction further.

Repair of tendons is slow, probably due to the poor blood supply. Physiotherapy is given to try to increase the blood supply — ice,

ultrasound or friction may be helpful with graded exercise and stretching. NSAIDs are of value. Treatment of tendon ruptures may be conservative or surgical, depending on the site.

Injections should never be given into a tendon, as the increase in intratendon volume would collapse blood vessels, and impair blood supply further.

Peritendinitis and tenosynovitis

These conditions are due to overuse, the repetitive excursions of the tendon causing friction and resultant acute inflammation in surrounding tissues.

Where tendons run through a synovial tendon sheath, excessive friction causes acute tenosynovitis — the lining swells on the inner and outer layers of the sheath, producing swelling and pain, and crepitus on movement (see Fig. 4.3). Typical sites for this are the tendons of abductor pollicis longus or extensor pollicis brevis (de Quervain's tenosynovitis), and the flexor and extensor tendons of the

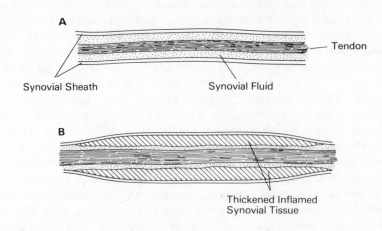

Fig. 4.3. A. Normal tendon in synovial sheath. B. Tenosynovitis.

wrist and ankle. It is particularly likely to occur when another structure impinges on the tendon, e.g. rowers are liable to tenosynovitis of extensor carpi radialis — the lesion develops where the muscle belly of abductor pollicis longus crosses the tendon. This muscle contracts when the oar is gripped tightly (novices especially tend to do this) and interferes with the extensor tendon as the wrist flexes and extends with each stroke. Runners sometimes get tenosynovitis of the dorsiflexors of the foot, due to the pressure from the tongue of a tightly laced shoe.

Other tendons do not run through tendon sheaths, but through loose connective tissue which allows free movement. Again, repetitive actions may cause friction and inflammation. An example of this is Achilles peritendinitis, which is particularly likely to occur in young runners and dancers.

Clinically, there is a warm sausage-shaped swelling around the tendon, with palpable crepitus on movement. It will settle with rest, ice treatment and NSAIDs. Infiltration of the area around the tendon with corticosteroid and local anaesthetic gives speedy resolution. Very occasionally chronic irritation in a synovial sheath may result in exuberant overgrowth of the synovial type tissue. Surgery to excise the swollen tissue, leaving the tendon sheath open and unsutured, gives good results.

LIGAMENT INJURIES

Acute tears

The majority of ligament injuries are partial tears, so that the ligament continues to stabilise the joint. There may be bruising and swelling, there is local tenderness over the ligament, and stressing the ligament gives pain. If the ligament is totally ruptured the joint is unstable. Total ruptures should be referred immediately to an orthopaedic surgeon, as they need suturing and/or prolonged immobilisation in plaster to allow healing.

If the ligament is partially intact and the joint is stable, it is best treated actively with physiotherapy. If treated with rest alone, the muscles acting on the joint waste rapidly, the proprioceptive mechanism becomes unresponsive, and the ligaments may shorten resulting after 3 weeks in a loss of range or even fixation of the joint, weak muscles and functional instability due to loss of proprioceptive feedback. Such a joint will require weeks or months of rehabilitation.

The aim of therapy is to achieve firm scar formation with a full range of movement, good muscle power and intact proprioceptive reflexes. Measures used to improve blood flow are ice, ultrasound and interferential treatment. Passive movements are started at once, progressing to active movements to prevent loss of range of movement. Graded exercises are used to build up the muscles around the joint, as they will take some of the stress off the ligament., Injuries to collateral ligaments of knee and ankle are common sports injuries. If there is much swelling and pain, crutches may be allowed for a few days, but the patient should weight-bear as soon as possible. The action of walking provides gentle movements to the joints and stimulates the proprioceptive end organs. Tubigrip or a light elastic bandage may be worn for some support without immobilisation — the pressure of this on the skin stimulates mechanoceptors and augments proprioception.

When weight-bearing is possible, exercises on the wobbleboard should be introduced — this again stimulates proprioceptive reflexes and prevents functional instability.

In most cases, sport can be resumed in 7–21 days, depending on the severity of the tear, once movements are full, with strong muscles and intact proprioceptive reflexes. A light T or stirrup strapping may be applied to the ankle — this again is effective because of stimulation of proprioceptive response through the skin. No player who needs to wear heavy strapping to compete is fit enough to compete — under these conditions, further injury to that joint or another is likely.

Chronic ligament injuries

Inadequately treated acute injuries result in weak muscles and loss of proprioception, and repetitive stresses to the ligament cause chronic scar tissue to develop. The symptoms are pain, instability and often swelling. On examination, there is local tenderness over the ligament, and sometimes palpable thickening. The ligament may have elongated. The muscles are weak, and fail to hold the bony surfaces in apposition, so there is joint laxity. Movement between the joint

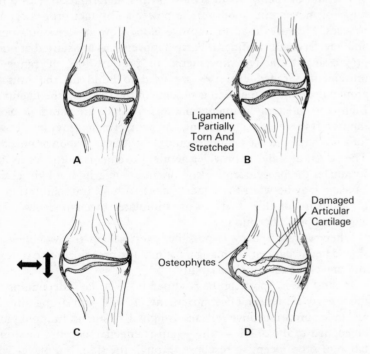

surfaces causes tugging on the insertion of capsule and ligament into the periosteum — in the long term this stimulates osteoblastic activity, with the formation of osteophytes. These are usually peripheral to the articular surfaces, but may mechanically limit the extremes of joint movement. They may also break off to form loose bodies — if intra-articular these will cause locking. Such changes can be clearly seen on X-ray — they are common in the ankles of professional football players (see Fig. 4.4).

The best management is to prevent this condition developing, by prompt and active treatment of acute ligament injuries. Chronic scar tissue will usually settle slowly with ice, ultrasound and friction. Sometimes local infiltration with corticosteroid and local anaesthetic may be helpful. The ligaments may have stretched and remain lax. Muscle power can be increased by resisted work, care being taken to maintain balance between agonists and antagonists. The proprioceptive responses will improve if maximally stimulated by wobbleboard and other exercises, but end organs which have become inactive through inflammation and disuse do not appear to recover. The bony changes are irreversible, and surgery is required to remove loose bodies which are causing locking. The ankle may become so disorganised with continued use that finally arthrodesis is the only measure to relieve pain.

Some ligaments may become stretched and inflamed due to repetitive stressing. For instance, the medial elbow ligament is stretched by javelin throwing if the elbow is not fully extended whilst throwing. This leads to pain and tenderness, and calcification may occur. In such a case correction of technique is essential for recovery.

Fig. 4.4. A. Diagrammatic joint B. Partial ligamentous tear. C. Lax ligaments and poor proprioception allowing play between bone ends. D. Osteoarthritic changes.

BURSITIS

A blow or repetitive friction to a bursa causes an increase in fluid production, and it becomes tense and swollen, and may impinge on surrounding structures.

The fluid can be aspirated and corticosteroid and local anaesthetic instilled. If it recurs this procedure may be repeated 2–3 times.

SYNOVITIS

The synovium responds to insult by becoming acutely inflamed, the resultant swelling and increased fluid production causing joint swelling. In acute synovitis, the over-production of fluid predominates, causing joint effusion, and the fluid can be palpated. In some chronic cases, the swelling is due to thickened synovium and there is a rubbery feel to the enlarged joint.

Trauma, infection or an underlying rheumatological condition may all cause an episode of synovitis, and it is important to make the correct diagnosis.

An acute blow, or prolonged running on a hard surface may both cause traumatic synovitis of the knee. This may occur in an otherwise normal joint, but such an injury may also precipitate an attack of synovitis in a person with underlying rheumatoid arthritis, ankylosing spondylitis or Reiter's syndrome. There may be a suggestive history of previous joint problems, but it may be the first attack. Anyone with synovitis that is persistent, has developed silently or after minimal trauma, or affects several joints, should be carefully examined for clinical signs of rheumatological disorder. Full blood count, erythrocyte sedimentation rate and Rose–Waaler tests should be done. The fluid should be aspirated and sent for cytology and culture. A synovial biopsy may be helpful in establishing a diagnosis.

Sometimes a blow appears to light up an infective synovitis, due to an organism of low pathogenicity, e.g. an atypical mycobacterium. For this reason, the fluid should always be cultured.

Another cause of persistent synovitis is mechanical irritation from loose bodies. If they are bony, they will show on X-ray. Cartilaginous ones will only show with arthrogram or arthroscopy. The advantage of arthroscopy is that any loose bodies can be removed, or a synovial biopsy can be taken for histology and culture.

INJURIES TO BONE

Fractures

Major fractures are usually taken direct to Accident and Emergency Centres, and do not present in Sports Injury Clinics, but occasionally a patient walks in with an unsuspected fracture, and this possibility should always be borne in mind. There is usually marked swelling and bruising, very localised bony tenderness and sometimes crepitus on movement of bone ends. An X-ray will usually confirm the diagnosis.

Fractures of phalanges or metacarpals are seen due to karate, boxing with untaped hands, cricket and hockey. Anyone who has fallen on an outstretched hand and is tender in the anatomical snuffbox should be suspected of a scaphoid fracture. These often do not show at first, so the wrist should be immobilised in a scaphoid plaster until 10 days later, when a repeat X-ray will show if there is a fracture or not.

At the ankle, the tip of the malleolus may be avulsed. This is particularly likely to occur on the medial malleolus, as the deltoid ligament is very strong. On the lateral side, it is usually the ligament which tears on inversion, but avulsion can occur, and if there is localised bony tenderness, an X-ray should be done (see Fig. 4.5).

If an injured joint swells immediately, or within 2 hours of injury, this must mean intra-articular haemorrhage, as an inflammatory exudate takes 8–12 hours to accumulate. X-rays will reveal a subchondral fracture — if there is none, the bleeding is from an intra-articular vascular structure e.g. in the knee the leash of vessels on the anterior cruciate ligament.

Young children have more flexible bones, and may present with partial thickness fractures of the long bones, following relatively minor trauma.

Fractures should be referred to an orthopaedic surgeon or fracture clinic — most require immobilisation.

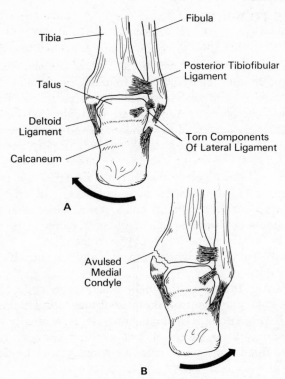

Fig. 4.5. Posterior views of ankle joint. A. Inversion sprain. B. Eversion sprain.

Stress fractures

These present quite frequently in Sports Injury Clinics. Most affect the bones of the leg and are due to running. Jarring on impact causes repetitive mechanical stress on the microtrabecular structure of bone. Eventually, a few of these give way, putting more stress on surrounding microtrabeculae, and thus it spreads to involve more bone, so that eventually this causes pain on exercise. Onset of pain may be sudden, but often there is a preceding story of 2–3 weeks intermittent pain, occurring on exercise and getting progressively worse. The metatarsals (especially 3rd and 4th), fibula and tibia are affected most often. Usually the fibular fractures are 1–2 inches above the lateral malleolus, and tibial fractures may be mid-shaft or 2–2½ inches below the tibial plateau. Sometimes they are bilateral. More rarely the femur or pubic ramus may be involved (see Fig. 4.6).

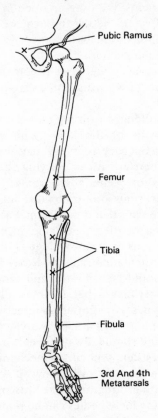

Fig. 4.6. Common sites of stress fractures.

Stress fractures are more likely to occur when running on hard surfaces rather than turf. They often occur within 2–3 weeks of starting to run, or stepping up the mileage. Bone does not attain full mechanical strength till the age of about 20, and below this age stress fractures occur more readily. Women with low oestrogen levels have some degree of osteoporosis, and are more likely to sustain stress fractures. This is relevant in menopausal or post-menopausal women. It is also a factor in younger women who are training hard — under these conditions the normal menstrual cycle is suppressed. They have amenorrhoea, and low oestrogen levels may result in osteoporosis. This syndrome tends to develop as body weight and subcutaneous fat (which produces some oestrogen) are reduced. It is reversible.

Stress fractures are more likely to develop in bones at a mechanical disadvantages, due for example to overweight, or to structural abnormality, causing uneven distribution of stress, e.g. short first metatarsal, genu-varum or valgum, femora recurvatum or dysplasia of the hip. All these conditions predispose to stress fractures of the leg bones.

Stress fractures occasionally develop at other sites — e.g. the dorsal process of C7 ('clay-shovellers' fracture) may fracture with repetitive weight training or racquet sports, the pull of the fibres of trapezius providing the stress.

Spondylolysis, which usually affects L4 or 5, is a stress fracture of the pars interarticularis.

Occasionally a stress fracture may develop in an abnormal region of bone which may be benign or may be due to a malignant tumour — such lesions will be revealed on X-ray.

Typically, there is no pain at rest, but hopping or running on the spot will bring it on. There is a very localised bony tenderness, but stressing the bone does not produce pain (unless rarely the fracture is full-thickness). There may be palpable thickening, due to callus, if it is of some duration.

X-ray should be done partly to exclude other bony lesions. A recent or small stress fracture may not show, but usually after 10 days there is enough callus formation to show up on conventional X-ray.

The diagnosis is made readily with technetium scanning, which shows a localised hot spot. If thermography is available, this is also diagnostic in most cases, as it shows a localised hot spot, and has the advantage of being non-invasive. Stimulation with continuous ultrasound can also be used as a diagnostic test, as it causes local pain, but it seems this only occurs if the fracture has extended to the periosteal surface and is recent. Most stress fractures heal with rest from running as sole treatment — 3 weeks for a metatarsal, 6 weeks for fibula, 8–10 weeks for tibia. Very occasionally they do not heal and a period of immobilisation in plaster is then required.

Cartilage

Cartilage has no blood supply, and depends on diffusion of oxygen and nutrients from the surfaces. Not surprisingly, it is slow to heal.

Occasionally, cartilage is bruised, due to jarring, e.g. at wrist or elbow after a fall. There is tenderness on the joint line, but a normal X-ray. It may take up to 3 months to become non-tender again.

The meniscal cartilages in the knee are subjected to shearing stresses when the knee twists while weight-bearing. This may cause bruising only, but may cause tears or detach part of the margin. In these latter cases, the distorted or detached cartilage causes locking of the knee, because it gets trapped between the articular surfaces.

Bruised cartilage recovers slowly — ice, ultrasound and interferential treatment may be beneficial, and NSAIDs are helpful. If these fail, local hydrocortisone may be of use.

In the case of torn meniscal cartilage, the only treatment is surgical removal of detached fragments and trimming of partially detached portions.

Enthesopathies

This term refers to lesions caused by traction of muscles, tendons, ligaments or fascia on the periosteum. The periosteum is lifted off the underlying bone and responds by becoming inflamed and painful. If the condition is long-standing, periosteal new bone is laid down.

Common examples are lateral and medial epicondylitis at the elbow — tennis and golf elbows respectively. The common form of shin splints associated with tenderness (often bilateral) of the middle third of the medial border of the tibia is due to the calf muscles tugging indirectly via the fascia from which they arise, and which is itself inserted into the medial border of tibia. Another example is plantar fasciitis, where the calcaneal insertion of the plantar fascia becomes inflamed — often a calcaneal spur develops.

Enthesopathies may be due simply to local stressing due to sport or other activities, but they are also a feature of the HLA 27 associated arthropathies. If an individual has more than one of these conditions, this possibility should be explored.

Osteochondritis

This term is used somewhat imprecisely to cover a group of disorders affecting bone ends. Mechanical stress appears to be a factor in their aetiology, and they occur most frequently in children and teenagers, whose bones are still growing, and where the growth plate is present. Many of these conditions have been dignified with eponymous names.

ISCHAEMIC OSTEOCHONDRITIS

Some of the conditions are due to ischaemia causing bone necrosis. These are nearly all due to trauma damaging the blood supply — examples of this are necrosis of the femoral head following a fracture through the neck of the femur, and necrosis of the distal part of the scaphoid following a fracture through the body.

CHILDHOOD AND ADOLESCENT OSTEOCHONDRITIS

Another group occurs in children and teenagers, and is characterised by necrotic changes in the ossification centre. There is no fracture, but trauma may nevertheless be relevant, as the condition occurs particularly in physically active children. There may also be a genetic element, as some families contain several similar cases.

Stress from overactivity may cause local ischaemia, which results in death of bone cells. Experimentally, it has been shown osteocytes can survive only 12 hours without oxygen, whereas chondrocytes can survive for 60 hours. Histologically there is a patchy appearance, with areas of bone necrosis and resorption, and other areas where regeneration appears to be underway.

The cases who present to their doctors complain of pain which may be severe (but there are reports of silent cases being found on routine X-rays). There is local tenderness over the affected bone and pain on movement. X-ray changes are slow to develop, and show increased density with apparent collapse of the bone. Later the density decreases and the bone may re-expand over many months. There is often some residual deformity. Examples of this are Kienboeck's disease (osteochondritis of carpal lúnate), Köehler's disease (tarsal navicular), Freiberg's disease (metatarsal head — usually the second), Perthes' disease (femoral head), and Scheuermann's disease of the vertebrae.

The X-ray changes are typical when they develop, but until they do, care must be taken to exclude other causes, in particular infection.

Management consists of physical rest of the part until recovery is complete. Non-weight-bearing exercise such as swimming should be encouraged.

AVULSION OSTEOCHONDRITIS

This group of disorders is due to pulling on tendons or muscle insertions, disrupting an underlying growth plate which is a weak point. The conditions are again most common in physically active children. There may be radiological changes in the bone in more severe cases, which may give some residual deformity in later life. In milder cases, the X-rays remain normal. There is local tenderness and often swelling. The condition settles spontaneously with rest, but may recur until growth stops and the growth plate is replaced by bone.

Osgood–Schlatter disease is due to avulsion of the tibial tubercle by the patellar tendon, and occurs particularly in keen footballers (on the kicking leg) and bilaterally in basketball players, but also in runners and jumpers.

Sever's disease is due to avulsion at the calcaneal insertion of the Achilles tendon. The apophysis of the iliac crest may be damaged by traction from the obliquus externus abdominus — a muscle which is used in running, particular when the arms are swung across the trunk.

OSTEOCHONDRITIS DISSECANS

In this condition, fragments of articular cartilage with underlying bone detach from the joint surface and form loose bodies in the joint. It occurs particularly on convex articular surfaces, e.g. capitulum of the humerus, proximal surface of the talus, and the femoral condyles.

It is usually related to trauma, occurs in the late teens and twenties, and is commoner in males.

If free in the joint space, the loose bodies cause recurrent locking and effusions. The cartilage bathed in synovial fluid may continue to grow, but the bone tends to degenerate.

On X-ray the fragments of detached bone can be seen and the site from which they have detached (if this is recent). Sometimes undisplaced fragments rejoin with surrounding bone. The fragments may be single, but are often multiple.

Treatment is surgical — it may be possible to replace a recently detached fragment. As time goes by, the cartilage on the fragment continues to grow, and the site of detachment may heal, rendering this impossible. Loose bodies should be removed. Sometimes more develop and need further surgery.

LESIONS OF NERVES

Neuropraxia

A direct blow or prolonged stretching of a nerve may cause temporary ischaemia, with death of the nerve fibres, causing sensory and motor changes. The cell bodies in the spinal cord are unaffected and the continuity of the nerve sheath is maintained so that eventually the fibres regrow and sensation and power return.

The common peroneal nerve may be injured by a kick on the top of the fibula, or if the squatting position is maintained for a long period it may stretch the nerve around the fibular neck, causing ischaemia and neuropraxia. Recovery occurs in time. An electromyogram will confirm the diagnosis and give some indication of time of recovery. Splinting may be necessary to control foot drop until reinnervation occurs, followed by strengthening exercises.

Similarly, the radial nerve may be injured by a blow to the upper arm, and the ulnar nerve by being stretched around the olecranon, e.g. cricket bowlers.

Entrapment neuropathies

Some peripheral nerves run through narrow channels between bone and ligaments, or under retinacula. In these situations, any swelling or increased pressure may compress the nerve, causing pain or paraesthesiae or weakness, or a combination of these. A few of these conditions may occur in athletes. The carpal tunnel syndrome may be precipitated by excessive movements of the wrist, causing some local hyperaemia and swelling, and compressing the median nerve.

Similarly, the posterior tibial nerve may become compressed in the tarsal tunnel, giving pain and paraesthiae in the foot.

The lateral femoral cutaneous nerve emerges from under the lateral end of the inguinal ligament. Pressure in the groin at this point may irritate the nerve, causing paraesthesiae in the anterior thigh. Tight jeans or body armour may press on it and cause symptoms. Electromyography confirms the diagnosis. Removal of the cause, rest by splinting, and local steroid infiltration may reduce swelling and abolish symptoms. Rarely surgical decompression is necessary.

Nerve root lesions

Pressure on the spinal nerves in the region of the intervertebral foramina will give symptoms of pain, numbness and paraesthesiae or weakness, or a mixture of these, in the structures supplied by that nerve. This is most often due to a prolapsed vertebral disc compressing the nerve root at this point.

The symptoms may be unilateral, but a posterior prolapse will affect both intervertebral foramina at that level, causing bilateral symptoms — a potentially dangerous condition as it may be followed by massive posterior prolapse with card compression.

In the cervical region, the symptoms are felt in shoulders, arms or back of scalp. In the lumbar region, the L4/L5 and L5/L6 discs are most often involved, causing sciatica.

There is usually accompanying pain and stiffness in the neck or back, but sometimes this is absent, or the patient has omitted to mention it. Careful physical examination will usually demonstrate some limitation of spinal movement, and X-rays may reveal narrowed disc spaces or osteophytes.

The treatment is that of the spinal problem — see below.

5
Some General Effects
on the Athlete and Performance

An individual's response to exertion, likelihood of sustaining injury and rapidity of recovery are influenced by various factors. Age and fitness are of major importance. Environmental factors can also be of relevance, particularly in endurance events. These are discussed briefly here, as the personnel of the Sports Injury Clinic may be asked to help organise such events. Finally there are some systemic effects of exertion for which an athlete may seek advice.

AGE

Age affects performance, injury rate and rate of recovery. There are probably many reasons for this, but two predominant ones are altering psychological attitudes, and changes in consistency and reactivity at the tissue level.

Mental attitudes to sport and psychological motivation vary between individuals, but certain general patterns exist.

The competitive urge seems to develop around the age of 8–10. It is unusual for young children to be particularly competitive, but the urge to win becomes apparent in early puberty, and tends to become more marked with increasing success. The enthusiasm of parents and coaches may add to the adolescent's endogenous drive and there is an all-too-real danger of excessive training and competing overtaxing immature skeletal tissues. Once growth has ceased, this becomes less of a problem. Whilst peak physical fitness occurs between 18–25 years, performance at endurance events seems to go on improving into the mid-thirties, and is probably in part due to increased patience and application. Motor skills, including eye-hand (or foot-ball) co-ordination develop during childhood and adolescence in all individuals, and can be improved with teaching and practice even late in life, and once acquired tend to persist in a gratifying way. Inherent, probably genetic factors underlie the marked variations in potential between individuals.

Increasing motivation and co-ordination put varying stresses on the connective tissues, which mature at different ages. Muscle can tolerate stress well from an early age, and muscle strains are not a problem in children and teenagers. During the adolescent growth spurt, there may be problems with poor muscle co-ordination as the child goes through a temporary gawky and clumsy stage, and this may cause problems due to poor muscle balance, e.g. patello-femoral syndrome, tight hamstrings, foot pain due to poor intrinsic muscles.

Muscle strength peaks around the age of 20, and in the late teens and twenties muscle injuries are usually due to clear-cut insults such as direct trauma, or lack of adequate warm-up and stretching. With increasing age changes occur in muscle, so that they tear more easily and bleed more profusely. For example, spontaneous partial rupture of calf muscles on sudden effort is rare before the mid-thirties, but after this age is quite common, especially whilst playing squash or tennis: activities requiring frequent sudden bursts of activity and changes of direction. Such injuries are often accompanied by quite disproportionate intramuscular bleeding. The presence of a quantity of blood in the muscle belly causes pain and limitation of movement, and delays recovery.

Tendons are very strong relative to other tissues at all ages, but especially so in children. Injuries to tendons themselves are very rare, but apophysitis due to traction of tendon on relatively soft bone, or actual avulsion of bone, are a frequent problem in competitive children and remain so until growth stops. Peritendinitis due to inflammation of the connective tissue around the tendon may also occur with overuse, e.g. at the shoulder (usually the supraspinatus tendon) or the Achilles tendon at the ankle in children.

Ligaments resemble tendons in being relatively strong in children. If stressed they will tend to avulse bone rather than tear, e.g. lateral and medial collateral ligaments of the ankle if stressed will tend to avulse the malleolus. (In adults the medial or deltoid ligament tends to remain stronger than bone, but the lateral collateral ligament is relatively less strong, and eventually tears rather than detach the lateral malleolus.) If a child falls and twists or dislocates the elbow, the medial ligament usually avulses the medial epicondyle of the humerus.

During the adolescent growth spurt, injuries to ligaments are more likely to occur if muscle co-ordination is poor, as the normal postural reflexes fail to cause effective agonist-antagonist interaction to protect moving joints.

In middle age, early osteoarthritic changes begin to develop. The bony surfaces of joints change shape as a result of wear and tear, articular cartilage may degenerate on weight-bearing surfaces, intra-articular fibrocartilages wear or undergo cystic change, and osteophytes may form peripherally due to repetitive pulling on capsule or ligaments. These changes mean the joint surfaces lose congruity, there is more play between them, and they are more easily displaced by outside forces. Thus the ligaments tend to get stressed and torn. Some compensation for this can be achieved by strengthening the surrounding muscles, which will then help to hold the joint surfaces in congruity.

The mechanical strength of bones is low in children; ground substance is less dense and contains less calcium salts than in adults, but there is a high content of collagen, and they are therefore relatively flexible. If bent, an adult's bone will snap and break clean through, but a child's bone bends, and the typical greenstick fracture occurs in which there is only a partial thickness break.

In children and adolescents, the reduced strength of the bone shaft means they are more liable to stress fractures, particularly with long-distance running. Children's running events should be of limited distance, depending on the age group, and they should not run marathons until over 18 years old.

Even more vulnerable than the shafts of the bone are the epiphyses. The highly cellular and vascular growing plates are very susceptible to jarring and repetitive trauma, which causes osteochondritis. There is ischaemia and death of osteoblasts, and physical disruption of the architecture. With rest and time, there is usually recovery, but the growth plate may remain distorted, so that the epiphysis becomes misshapen and liable to mechanical troubles and early onset of osteoarthritis in later life.

The joints are more flexible in early years, due to pliability of the ligaments and tendons, and these structures may be stressed if the child is trained too hard and encouraged to adopt extreme postures. This is mostly a problem with dancers and gymnasts in the under 10 age group, as children of promise tend to be selected early and trained hard from a tender age.

Osteochondritis dissecans usually occurs in teenagers, and is associated with trauma and physical activity. Pieces of bone and overlying cartilage become detached from usually convex bone surfaces, e.g. femoral condyles, capitulum of humerus and upper surface of talus. These loose bodies may cause immediate symptoms or lurk in recesses of the joint, and only later get trapped between articular surfaces, causing locking and instability. They are often multiple.

Mention has already been made of the degenerative changes of osteoarthritis which develop in middle-aged joints. Similar changes develop earlier in joints subjected to excessive mechanical abuse, e.g. ankles of professional footballers, in which repeated and often inadequately treated ligament sprains cause loss of proprioceptive feedback, lax ligaments and increased play between joint surfaces. The articular cartilage degenerates and osteophytes form at the site of ligament and capsular insertions. Previous damage also predisposes to early osteoarthritis, e.g. Perthes' disease of the hip, or a

Table 5.1. Age-related spinal injuries

Age	Injuries
Juvenile	Hyperextension injuries of ligaments
	Spondylolysis
Adolescent	Spondylolysis — spondylolisthesis
	Scheuermann's disease
	Vertebral body fractures
Young adult	Stress fracture
	Old Scheuermann's disease
	Spondylolysis — spondylolisthesis
	Prolapsed intervertebral disc
	Congenital abnormalities
	Spina bifida occulta
	Abnormalities of segmentation
	Partially lumbarised S1
	Ankylosing spondylitis
Middle-aged	Lumbar spondylosis
	Disc space narrowing and osteophytes
	Osteoarthritis of apophyseal joints
	Ligamentous laxity and weak muscles

partially slipped femoral epiphysis. In the knee, lax cruciates and total menisectomy both interfere with the mechanics of the joint and lead to early degenerative changes.

The spine suffers different types of injuries at different ages, see Table 5.1.

Hyperextension of the spine occurs repeatedly in gymnastics, modern dance movements and butterfly stroke. Compressive forces are applied to the spine in weight-lifting and training, rowing, trampolining and in rugby scrums. Repetitive jarring is particularly likely to occur in long-distance running, especially on roads.

In the juvenile and adolescent cases, the injury is usually caused by sport, whereas in the middle-age group, a pre-existing problem may be aggravated by excessive exercise. This is likely to be associated with structural changes in the spine. The actively growing child has an epiphyseal cartilage plate on the superior and inferior surfaces of the vertebral body, which seem to be weaker than the annulus fibrosus of the intervertebral disc, so forces applied to the disc–vertebral complex damage the growth plate, causing an osteochondritis — Scheuermann's disease. Once the epiphyseal plates have ossified and fused with the body of the vertebra at somewhere between 18 and 20 years of age, the vertebral end-plate becomes much stronger, and in adults overloading tends to cause tears of the annulus fibrosus with protrusion of the nucleus pulposus (see Fig. 5.1).

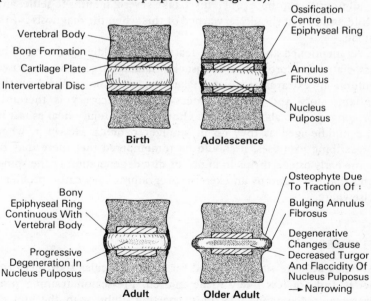

Fig. 5.1. Structural changes in the spine from birth to old age.

AGE AND RESPONSE TO TREATMENT

On the whole, athletes are well-motivated and compliant with treatment regimes. They may be initially reluctant to take time off training or sport if this is necessary, but if the reasons are explained clearly, together with the course and likely duration of treatment, and the disadvantages of not doing this, they are usually very co-operative. Wherever possible, some form of exercise should be recommended which will not exacerbate the injury, but will allow general fitness to be maintained.

One group of injuries which seems slow to respond to rest and treatment is bony problems in children and adolescents. This group includes the osteochondritides and avulsion injuries, and the delay is probably connected with bone growth. Whatever the reason, it is not at all unusual for these problems to take several months to settle, and child and parent should be warned of this when the diagnosis is first made.

As mentioned above, muscle tears in the middle-aged tend to be associated with profuse intramuscular haemorrhage. This increased volume of extravasated blood takes longer to be resolved by the inflammatory and healing processes, and recovery is therefore prolonged up to about 6 weeks. Other types of injury heal as fast in the middle-aged as they do in younger patients. However, when prescribing exercises, it should be remembered that there may be some early osteoarthritis in joints, or disc degeneration in the spine, and that too vigorous an exercise programme may cause problems elsewhere.

FITNESS

Athletes who are fit and trained for their particular sport perform better and are less likely to be injured. Pre-season training programmes are organised by most sporting clubs, with the aim of bringing their members to match fitness by the beginning of the season. If a player has been off because of an injury, it is very important to train properly to regain fitness before competing again. This concept of fitness for a particular sport is also important for people engaged in holiday activities such as skiing and mountain walking and climbing. Pre-vacation preparation with some general endurance training and specific exercises avoids initial fatigue and stiffness, so that the holiday is enjoyable from the start. General training improves utilisation of oxygen by training the cardiovascular and respiratory systems — this is achieved by aerobic activities such as walking, running, cycling and swimming, and the pace and distance should be increased gradually, according to the age and physical habitus of the individual, to reach a level appropriate to the intended activity.

WARMING UP

Warming up is particularly important before contact sports and short-burst activities. It means the player performs well from the outset and even more important, is less liable to muscle and other soft tissue injuries. The process involves stretching muscles so that they become supple and well-perfused with blood, putting the joints through a full range of movement, jogging to increase cardiac output, some psyching up for the contest — generally getting body and mind into a state of readiness. In team sports, there is often a team warming-up session, but in other sports it is up to the individual.

In general, about 15 minutes should be spent warming up, and the processes should be completed not more than 5 minutes before the start. If the start is delayed, further warming up should be done. In cold weather, the process takes longer, as muscles tend to be stiffer.

Following a soft tissue injury, the player should be given specific stretching exercises to add to the usual regime — this is very helpful in preventing a recurrence.

INTERCURRENT INFECTIONS

It is unwise to train hard and compete when suffering from an infection. Performance will be off-peak, any fever will be increased, so that in hot conditions there may be danger of hyperthermia, and there is more likelihood of sustaining an injury (probably because judgement and co-ordination are sub-optimal). If there is a respiratory tract infection, symptoms are likely to be aggravated by the increased ventilation rate of exercise, which will move more air, possibly cold and dry, over the inflamed mucosae. The myalgia accompanying virus infections (due to interferon production) is exacerbated by exertion. Finally, apparently mild virus infections may be accompanied by a viral myocarditis, which may cause no symptoms when resting, but the increased heart-rate of exercise may precipitate ventricular fibrillation and sudden death.

Infectious mononucleosis is not uncommon in the teens and early twenties. It may have a prolonged course, and exacerbate the pain and stiffness of soft tissue injuries, and delay recovery. When someone in this age group takes longer than expected to recover from an injury, and seems generally below par, it is worthwhile doing a blood count and mono-spot or Paul–Bunnell test, to see if this is the problem.

ENVIRONMENTAL FACTORS

During endurance events such as running, cycling, walking and cross-country skiing, or long team games such as football or hockey, the players are exposed to environmental factors which may have a marked effect.

Extremes of temperature, humidity and altitude may predispose to systemic reactions to over-exertion. Such factors should always be taken into account when planning and supervising sporting events.

Dehydration

During exercise fluid is lost by sweating and by evaporation from the respiratory tract. If the event is prolonged and taking place at high ambient temperatures, this loss is increased up to 1 litre per hour. Sweat contains electrolytes, particularly sodium, which are also lost. Depletion of fluid and electrolytes contributes to hyperthermia (see below) and leads to circulatory collapse. A man weighing 65 kg has body fluids of about 40 litres. He can lose up to 2 litres of fluid without ill-effects, but a loss of 5 litres causes symptoms including confusion, and a loss of 6–8 litres can be fatal. Serious effects of fluid depletion can be prevented by administering adequate fluid and electrolytes at intervals during the event. Some sugar may be given, but it should be well-diluted or it causes delay in gastric emptying and nausea. Various proprietary mixtures are available which provide a balanced mixture of sugar and electrolytes, usually with a citrus flavour. The volume required depends on the severity and duration of exercise and on the prevailing temperature and wind. For instance, in hot conditions walkers are advised to carry and drink one gallon of fluid daily. They can reduce fluid loss by resting, in shade if possible, and avoiding exertion during the hottest part of the day. Runners would lose fluid at a greater rate because of increased exertion and respiratory rate, but would be exercising for shorter periods than walkers. Officials in charge of an event should estimate fluid and electrolyte requirements for the prevailing conditions, set up refreshment posts and ensure all competitors drink their ration.

Temperature changes

HYPERTHERMIA

During exercise, muscles generate heat, which is lost as latent heat of vaporisation by sweating and evaporation of water from the respiratory tract and by radiation from dilated blood vessels in the skin.

Sweating is the most important of these, and provided the individual drinks enough, the core temperature can be kept normal by these means. In humid conditions, heat loss from sweating is much less effective. If the individual is fluid-depleted, it is also impaired. Human beings do not have an accurate thirst-drive, and need to be encouraged to drink adequate amounts under extreme conditions. In the presence of dehydration, the core temperature rises and hyperthermia develops. Anyone with a mild febrile illness already is likely to have a raised core temperature, and should not undertake vigorous exercise.

Temperature regulation is less efficient in women, who do not sweat as profusely as men, but as partial compensation vasodilate more, and become very flushed. (There seems to be some physiological basis to the saying 'horses sweat, men perspire and ladies merely glow'!) Women are likely to develop a raised core temperature, and therefore perform less well than men in hot conditions, and more easily develop hyperthermia or heatstroke.

As the core temperature rises above 38–39°C, symptoms develop; in addition to flushing and sweating, there is headache, tachycardia, abdominal cramps and physical performance deteriorates. Effective treatment depends on lowering the core temperature; rest from physical exertion, preferably in shade, drinking cold drinks, sponging with cold water or immersion in water if available. Aspirin and paracetamol by mouth affect the thermoregulatory centre, stimulating sweating and lowering core temperature.

Heatstroke occurs when the core temperature rises above 40°C. There is irreversible damage to the central nervous system. Increasing confusion progresses to coma, and there may be convulsions. Hypothalamic damage interferes with normal heat regulation mechanisms, so that sweating and vasodilation are turned off. The skin is dry and pale, and there is circulatory collapse. Further rise in temperature results in permanent damage or death. Heatstroke is a medical emergency, and immediate cooling is required.

HYPOTHERMIA

On land: Hypothermia due to exposure can occur in conditions above freezing temperatures if loss of body heat is increased by wet and windy conditions. Extreme physical exertion may generate enough heat to balance this, but as the individual tires and slows down, heat production declines. Chilling of the limbs causes clumsiness and slowness, and further heat loss. The core temperature then starts to fall. Cooling of the brain causes loss of judgement and confusion. As the core temperature drops to 30–32°C, there is loss of consciousness. If the individual remains exposed, death usually occurs in 1–2 hours after loss of consciousness. The temperature continues to fall and at 24–26°C, ventricular fibrillation occurs. However, these changes are potentially reversible, if rewarming can be achieved.

Such conditions may affect fell-walkers and marathon runners when the temperature is under 8°C, if it is rainy and windy in addition. Adequate clothing consisting of several layers should be worn, with a waterproof covering to keep them dry. Headgear is important, as 10% of heat loss occurs from the head. Someone wearing soaking clothes has no more insulation than when naked. Marathon runners may think they produce enough heat to allow them to keep warm in a singlet and shorts, but in cold conditions they should wear long sleeves and trousers. More clothes or thermal blankets should be put on them if they stop or slow down. Walkers need more insulation from clothing, as they generate less heat and are exposed for longer at a time.

Any individual who begins to stagger or seems drowsy should be sheltered immediately from the wind by some means — this may mean putting up a tent, or wrapping them in a thermal blanket or bivvy bag. A young, healthy person can be re-warmed quickly by immersion in a warm bath. Out on the moors, the only effective method of warming may be for another member of the party to get in the bivvy bag with the victim. If the victim has lost or is losing consciousness, time is short — re-warming so that consciousness is regained must be achieved before continuing evacuation.

In water: Someone falling into water may drown, but if able to swim or supported by a buoyancy aid, death from hypothermia is a danger. Immersion in water at 0°C causes death within an hour, sometimes after only 15–20 minutes. Immediate death due to myocardial ischaemia and ventricular fibrillation may occur due to coronary artery spasm.

In water at 15°C most people survive up to 6–8 hours. Survival is prolonged if they are wearing a lot of clothes, preferably with a waterproof outside layer, as this provides good insulation. It is also advantageous to keep still, as moving about increases heat dissipation.

Long-distance swimmers may spend up to 18 hours in water of this temperature, but they are a highly selected group. They tend to be fat, with a thick subcutaneous insulating fat layer, and as they are taking vigorous exercise, their muscles generate a great deal of heat. If they tire and slow down, they tend to develop hypothermia.

High altitude

High altitude causes problems due to low oxygen pressure, increased evaporation of water from the respiratory tract and possibly extremes of temperature. Individuals vary in their sensitivity, children, adolescents and the elderly being particularly likely to be affected. Most people notice some breathlessness on exertion if they are suddenly taken up above 2 000 m, for instance by aeroplane or cable-car. The more susceptible develop headache and nausea. These symptoms settle over 24–48 hours, as acclimatisation occurs, or can be prevented by a more gradual ascent. Above 6 000 m, there may be some confusion and loss of judgement, due to hypoxaemia. Pulmonary oedema may develop suddenly, and requires immediate evacuation to a lower altitude.

Acetazolamide is useful in preventing altitude sickness, though side-effects such as paraesthiae may be a nuisance.

People over 35 years of age run a serious risk of cerebral Chromhosis at high altitude and should not go above 6 000 m.

SOME SYSTEMIC EFFECTS OF OVEREXERTION

Haematuria

Occasionally frank haematuria occurs following extreme exertion. Routine urine testing of marathon runners shows albuminuria and microsopic haematuria in almost everyone. It is thought to be renal in origin, resolves spontaneously and is of no serious significance.

March haemoglobinuria

This is a rare condition, affecting mostly males, in which haemoglobinuria occurs for a few hours, following vigorous exercise, such as walking or running on hard surfaces. It does not occur with cycling or swimming, and it is believed to be due to physical trauma to normal red cells in the blood vessels in the soles of the feet.

Attacks tend to occur shortly after taking up running, or when resuming after a break, and particularly affect heavy-footed individuals. Several attacks may occur, and then the condition resolves. The presenting complaint is of passing red or dark urine after exercise for a few hours. Occasionally nausea and vague pains in the abdomen, back or legs may be noticed. Only rarely is the individual clinically anaemic or jaundiced, as less than 1% of the red cells are haemolysed during an attack.

Examination of urine reveals haemoglobin and sometimes haemosiderin with small amounts of albumin. The red cells are mechanically and osmotically normal, with no excess fragility.

The differential diagnosis is from haematuria due to local renal trauma, paroxysmal nocturnal haemoglobinuria and myoglobinuria (see below).

The symptoms are usually reduced by running on springy turf instead of roads, and by wearing running shoes with more resilient soles.

Paroxysmal nocturnal haemoglobinuria

This is an acquired condition in which the surface of the red cells alters so that complement may be fixed and cause lysis in the absence of antibody. Typically this occurs during sleep, but attacks may be precipitated by exercise (possibly associated with lowering of the blood pH) so that dark urine is passed after exercise.

These patients are often anaemic and clinically jaundiced. Examination of the urine shows haemoglobin. Diagnosis depends on demonstrating the red cell sensitivity to complement *in vitro*.

Myoglobinuria

Myoglobinuria occurs following extensive trauma to muscle as myoglobin is released from necrotic muscle fibres. It also occurs after exercise in people with primary muscle disease such as muscular dystrophy and some rare muscle enzyme abnormalities.

Myoglobin in the urine can be differentiated from haemoglobin by electrophoresis.

Disturbance of vision

AMBLYOPIA

Transient amblyopia occurring during or after exercise is usually due to hypotension. As soon as the perfusion of the cortex and retina returns to normal, e.g. on lying down, full vision returns.

FIELD DEFECTS

Transient visual field defects, e.g. scotoma or hemianopia may come on during strenuous exercise and go away spontaneously afterwards, only to recur on further exercise. This rare phenomenon is usually due to an early lesion of multiple sclerosis affecting the optic nerve. The rise in core temperature induced by exercise precipitates symptoms. The patient should be referred to a neurologist for full assessment, including visually evoked potentials.

Gastrointestinal reactions

Severe prolonged exercise may cause gastrointestinal symptoms. Some are due to the gut becoming relatively ischaemic as blood is diverted to muscles. Production of adrenalin and other stress-related factors may also be involved.

Gastric emptying is delayed, leading to nausea and sometimes vomiting. This can be reduced by not eating within 2 hours of an event, and drinking small quantities at intervals, instead of one large drink. It helps if the sugar content of the drink is low as sugar delays gastric emptying.

Rarely, Curling's ulcers, which are related to acute stress, form in the duodenum, causing haematemesis or melaena.

During long-distance events, some runners develop abdominal cramps and diarrhoea. They may need intravenous fluids and electrolytes.

Cardiovascular system

Normally physical effort causes an increased cardiac output by increasing the heart-rate and stroke volume. In individuals with ischaemic heart disease, the coronary flow may not be sufficient to supply adequate oxygen to the myocardium and an acute myocardial infarct may occur. In other people who have diffuse myocardial ischaemia, or in someone in whom a virus myocarditis complicates a systemic virus infection, ventricular fibrillation, or acute asystole may cause sudden death.

Trained athletes have a slow pulse and enlarged hearts. They have typical ECG changes which may be misinterpreted as being pathological.

Headache

Headache is one of the symptoms of hyperthermia (see above). The headache resolves as the core temperature drops, and is helped by aspirin or paracetamol.

Post-exertional migraine

Migrainous headaches may be precipitated by competitive events. The pre-event stress and excitement is probably a key factor in causing the underlying vascular changes, as it occurs with sprinting and short-burst activity as well as endurance events. It is commonest in people liable to migraine, but not confined to this group. The headache is typically unilateral and severe, and may be preceded by neurological prodromata. The attack may take 2–3 days to settle. Following an attack, the intracranial vessels may remain irritable, so that further attacks follow subsequent training sessions or competition. In this case, a few weeks rest from hard training and competition usually resolves the problem.

The differential diagnosis is from intracranial haemorrhage.

Intracranial haemorrhage

This is a rare concomitant of exertion and is almost always due to rupture of an abnormal blood vessel, for instance a berry aneurysm, haemangiomatous malformation or atheromatous vessel.

Section II

Regional Problems

DIAGNOSIS

Armed with a knowledge of anatomy, an understanding of the manner in which different tissues respond to injury and a clear history from the patient of what happened to provoke the injury, the examiner should have a good idea of a likely diagnosis before examining the patient. This should not of course prejudice the thoroughness of the examination, and sometimes there are unexpected findings. Examination follows the time-honoured routine of inspection, palpation and passive and active movement.

Inspection begins as the patient walks into the consulting room — age, body build, ease of movement (there may be a limp or obviously stiff back or neck), general bearing such as whether relaxed or in obvious pain, all furnish important information. The patient should then be asked where the injury is, what sport was involved, and to recall in as much detail as possible how it happened. For instance, if the injury was a collision with another player in a contact sport, it is important to know which body parts collided, in which way the player was forced, and in which direction twisting occurred if there were any rotary forces. This is particularly important with knee injuries, where the internal anatomy is complicated and difficult to evaluate thoroughly by clinical examination. A clear history suggests which structures have been stressed. If injury forced the patient to rotate to the right, while weight-bearing on a partially flexed right knee, foot locked by the studs into a muddy pitch, then stress will have been applied to the medial collateral ligament, medial meniscus and anterior cruciate ligament, and damage may have occurred in turn (in that order) to all of these structures. Evidence for this can be sought at examination.

If the injury affects a runner, the athlete should describe when symptoms first came on, and how they progressed, at what stage in the run, whether it has got worse subsequently, if the pain comes on earlier and more severely with subsequent runs, whether other activities such as walking or cycling or going up or down stairs elicit the symptoms. With runners it is also important to establish how far they run a week, how far at an outing, how long they have been doing it, any recent increase in mileage or speed, the type of surface run on, and the state of their running shoes.

Direct questions can be asked to furnish clues. Have there been previous injuries at the site — if so, when, and how long did recovery take? Does the joint lock? — this suggests the presence of a loose body. Does it give way? —this may be due to lax or torn ligaments, or to poor proprioception. If joint swelling occurred, how quickly did it come up after the injury? — if within 2 hours, this must mean a haemarthrosis and is due to either partial or complete rupture of a vascular intra-articular structure, or to a fracture in the joint surface, so X-rays are necessary. If pain follows the distribution of a dermatome or is bilateral and symmetrical, it may be referred from the spine, and the patient should be asked about pain in the spine currently or in the past, and if there is any tingling or numbness associated with the pain, which would indicate nerve root pressure.

Occasionally a pre-existing condition may be brought to light by an apparent sports injury. For instance, the late teens and early twenties are the peak ages at risk for osteosarcoma, and occasionally these tumours may present as a pathological fracture due to sport. The lower femur is most frequently involved. Occasionally chronic infections may present as a sports injury e.g. osteomyelitis, or septic arthritis. A small percentage of athletes with back pain turn out to have undiagnosed ankylosing spondylitis. Patients presenting with bilateral effusions of knees, ankles or less frequently other joints, may have Reiter's syndrome. These possibilities should always be borne in mind, and the relevant investigations done where necessary.

In a Sports Injury Clinic there is not time to do a full medical examination. However, it is important to assess general configuration. The patient should be stripped to underclothes and asked to stand barefoot, so an appraisal of body conformation can be done. General body build, height and degree of obesity determine the load put on the lower limbs, which may be inappropriate to the particular

BIRMINGHAM UNIVERSITY LIBRARY

sporting activity which has caused the injury. Spinal scoliosis, kyphosis or lordosis may be temporary due to muscle spasm, or may be structural and predispose to mechanical problems. Unequal leg length of more than one-quarter inch may cause problems in runners. The alignment of the lower limbs is especially important, and any malalignment may be of significance especially in sports involving a lot of running. Significant structural abnormalities in the feet are high medial arches (pes cavus), a pronated foot with low medial arch, a short first metatarsal (Morton's foot), hallux valgus, calcaneo-valgus or varus. Knee problems such as genu valgum or varum and a high or laterally dislocating patella are significant. Torsion of the femora may result in medially or laterally facing patellae, and this may be accompanied by anteversion of the femoral necks. The Q-angle is the angle of intersection of a line drawn from the anterior superior iliac spine through the midpoint of the patella with a line from the tibial tubercle drawn through the same point. It is considered abnormal if greater than 20° — such individuals are particularly liable to get patello-femoral syndrome with excessive running.

Another constitutional factor to look for is the degree of suppleness or stiffness. Hypermobile joints are more at risk.

This quick assessment should be followed by a detailed examination of the injured part. Inspection for swelling, redness, bruising or grazing, muscle wasting, bony configuration, or visible muscle spasm is aided by comparison with the normal side. The skin may feel hot due to inflammation. Palpation will find tender points. It is important to localise the depth of tenderness, i.e. subcutaneous, in muscle, ligament or tendons, or on bone, and its precise position within the affected structure. Muscle injury can be confirmed by doing resisted movements and eliciting pain at the site of tenderness. Any thickening or palpable mass should be noted. Chronic scar tissue in muscle tends to be palpable as nodules, and an intramuscular haematoma produces a large area of induration. Fluid in joints can be balloted. Distended bursae or other areas of localised fluid, e.g. a cyst in a resolving haematoma can be identified by moving the fluid between forefinger and thumb of one hand, and forefinger of the other hand. A palpable friction rub may be felt over areas of tenosynovitis or peritendinitis. Usually the patient has noticed a creaking sensation. Grating when bone is palpated suggests a fracture.

Joints should be examined thoroughly including those above and below the injury. An undiagnosed problem here may have contributed to injury. If the joint itself is injured, pain, impaired movement and instability are all significant. Range of movement and integrity of ligaments must be checked. If referred pain from the spine is suspected, the spine should be examined fully and any muscle spasm or impaired movement noted.

Leg length discrepancies should be noted — the measurement from the anterior superior iliac spine to the medial malleolus is recommended. Tendon reflexes, muscle power and sensation should be tested in the different dermatomes.

INVESTIGATION

Whenever a bony lesion is suspected an X-ray must be done. X-rays are also indicated in certain other circumstances, e.g. eversion sprains of the ankle where the strong deltoid ligament may avulse the medial condyle, in the investigation of patello-femoral pain, suspected osteochondritic conditions in children, and in older athletes where underlying osteoarthritis is suspected. If a joint is locking, it should be X-rayed to look for loose bodies. Special views may be required, and any bony loose bodies will be demonstrated. If these X-rays show nothing, the patient should proceed to an arthrogram, where the contrast medium will outline cartilaginous loose bodies, or if appropriate and available an arthroscopy may be done — this has the advantage that the loose body can be isolated and removed.

Spinal X-rays should be done whenever there is root pain and neurological symptoms, but also when there has been acute trauma to the spine — this is particularly important with the neck where there may be an unstable fracture and danger of tetraplegia. The cervical, dorsal or lumbar spine should also be X-rayed before any attempt is made to manipulate it — any contraindications such as tumours, fractures, osteoporosis or osteophytes protruding into intervertebral foramina can then be identified, and the danger of tetraplegia or paraplegia averted. Computed tomography will show the intervertebral discs and any prolapse. Stress fractures do not show up on routine X-rays if they are small or recent. They can be identified accurately using a technetium bone scan. They can also be identified almost as reliably by thermography.

Occasionally blood tests are required. A full blood count with differential white cell count may indicate bacterial or viral infection, and a raised ESR is suggestive of either extensive inflammation or a systemic problem. Where relevant, tests for rheumatoid factor, complement levels, immune complexes, uric acid and HLA-typing may be done.

Any athlete who has been struck in the loin should have his urine examined for red cells, as the kidneys may be bruised.

Fluids aspirated from joints, bursae or anywhere else should always be sent for culture in case they are infected.

As a result of the examination with or without further investigations, a diagnosis can usually be made which specifies the site and nature, size and cause of the injury. Occasionally an overuse injury may only produce symptoms after prolonged activity and there may be no abnormal findings when the patient comes to the clinic. In this case the patient should be sent off to run (or pursue whatever other activity causes the problem) until symptoms appear and then come back for re-examination.

Once the diagnosis is made, appropriate treatment can be started promptly, or if necessary the patient may be referred to the relevant specialist, e.g. orthopaedic surgeon, eye surgeon, ENT or dental surgeon.

In the following chapters specific injuries will be described by body part, and structurally from outside in, i.e. skin, muscle, tendon, ligaments, bursae, joints, bones and nerves.

6
The Foot

NAILS AND SKIN

Subungual haematoma

This is usually due to running or walking downhill in shoes or boots with a tight toe box. It may be acutely painful at first, because swelling occurs in a restricted space under the nail. It usually subsides with relief of pressure, but if very painful the pressure can be released by making holes in the nail with a red hot pin — a large safety pin is recommended, as the hole produced is large enough to allow extravasated blood to escape. It must be kept clean and painted with iodine to avoid infection. Shoes with more toe room should then be used. Almost always the nail bed is affected, and the nail comes off at a later date, and then regrows.

Ingrowing toenail

This affects the big toe, and is associated with footwear with inadequate toe room, or with cutting toe nails down too far at the sides. It frequently becomes infected. Treatment involves eradicating infection, for which systemic antibiotics are usually necessary, followed by allowing the nail to regrow, and subsequently cutting it straight across. Shoes with more roomy toes should be worn. Occasionally, partial or total avulsion of the nail is necessary.

Prominent or long nails

These may dig into the adjacent toe and cause excoriation of the skin. This is cured by trimming the nail and putting a plaster dressing on the injured toe.

Athlete's foot

This is due to a fungal dermatophyte infection and is commonest between 4th and 5th digits, but it may spread to the other interdigital clefts and the plantar surface. It is very common in mild form. It can be treated with fungicidal creams such as clotrimazole 1% or econazole nitrate 1% or miconazole nitrate 2%. Foot hygiene, with careful drying between toes helps prevent further attacks.

MUSCLE

Intrinsic foot muscle strains

There are few muscles in the feet, and acute strains are rare. However, weakness of intrinsic foot muscles (interossei and lumbricals) is a common condition, which is probably related to wearing shoes habitually — it does not occur in people who go barefoot. As the muscles waste from chronic disuse, the metatarsals tend to splay apart and the transverse arch across the heads of the metatarsals drops. The foot becomes broader, and may stretch the plantar fascia, which aches. In addition, the second, third and fourth metatarsal heads touch down and become bruised and tender. They may impinge on the nerves going into the toes and this causes a disagreeable neuralgic pain called metatarsalgia which radiates into the toes. After repeated trauma, the nerve may develop a neuroma.

Claw toe deformities may develop due to imbalance between interossei and lumbricals.

In addition to these problems, the altered foot mechanics may cause overuse problems at the knee.

On examination the foot looks broad and there are hollows

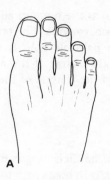 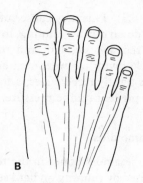

Fig. 6.1. A. Normal foot. B. Foot with weak intrinsic muscles, resulting in a broader foot, gaps between the toes, and wasted muscles making the tendons appear prominent.

between the metatarsals, which contrasts with the 'meaty' appearance of a healthy forefoot (Fig. 6.1). The metatarsal heads are tender. The patient cannot contract the intrinsic muscles and narrow the foot. A neuroma may be palpable as a tender knot on the plantar surface.

Treatment consists of exercises to build up the intrinsic foot muscles. Two to three sessions of faradic foot baths teach voluntary control and the patient can then practise tightening and relaxing the muscles at regular intervals. As recovery occurs (over 3–4 weeks), the foot becomes narrower and more muscular and the transverse arch reforms. If a neuroma persists it may need surgical treatment.

FASCIA

Plantar fasciitis

The plantar fascia becomes diffusely tender if traumatised unduly, e.g. by the metatarsal heads when the intrinsic foot muscles are weak (see above) or by running in thin soles on a hard or rough surface. This settles with rest and can be prevented by maintaining good foot muscles, and wearing thick resilient soles. Diffuse or calcaneal fasciitis is also associated with ankylosing spondylitis and Reiter's syndrome.

Plantar fascial tear

The plantar fascia may be partly detached from its origin on the calcaneum causing local pain and tenderness, aggravated by weight-bearing or running (see Fig. 6.2). Feet with pes cavus are particularly liable to this, as the plantar fascia is continuously under tension. The tear may be caused by jumping or stepping down or an unexpected step forcing the foot suddenly into dorsiflexion when the agonist and antagonist muscles are not acting. It may also be caused by running in unusually low heels. Detachment is partial, but it may take a long time to heal. Physiotherapy using ultrasound and frictions is helpful, and a course of non-steroidal anti-inflammatory drugs should be given for a minium of 2 weeks. Wearing heels of at least ¾–1 inch reduces the pull on the plantar fascial origin, and a heel pad made of one of the shock-absorbing polymers may be helpful. The patient should not run or jump until it is soundly healed, which may take 6 weeks or even longer. If it persists despite these measures, it may be

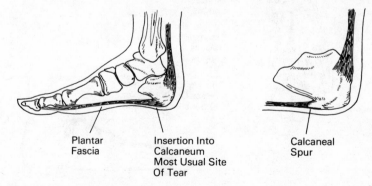

Plantar   Insertion Into   Calcaneal
Fascia   Calcaneum   Spur
                 Most Usual Site
                 Of Tear

Fig. 6.2. Detachment of plantar fascia from calcaneum.

because so much chronic scar tissue has formed that proper union is prevented. In this case, a course of three injections of 50 mg hydrocortisone with some local anaesthetic injected right into the tender region, at a minimum of 2-weekly intervals can be tried.

The significance of calcaneal spurs is uncertain. They are often present in the other symptom-free heel as well, and it may be that they merely form in response to tugging on the plantar fascia and indicate a predisposition to sustain a plantar fascial tear rather than being associated with the tear itself.

TENDONS

Tenosynovitis of dorsiflexor tendons

If shoes or boots are laced too tightly, they press on the dorsiflexor tendons as they run through synovial sheaths on top of the foot (see Fig. 6.3). This may cause sufficient friction, as the tendons slide up and down during running, to cause acute tenosynovitis. The tendons are red and swollen, and there may be a palpable rub. It settles quickly with ice treatment and avoiding tight lacing. If the athlete likes tightly laced shoes, a foam pad behind the tongue of the shoe will prevent undue pressure.

Sesamoiditis

The sesamoid bones in the tendon of flexor hallucis longus may be bruised by running on hard surfaces, especially in boots with the stud placed just under the metatarso-phalangeal joint. The tenderness is localised over the sesamoid bone (see Fig. 6.4). It usually recovers with ice and ultrasound, and a pad to redistribute pressure away from the bones.

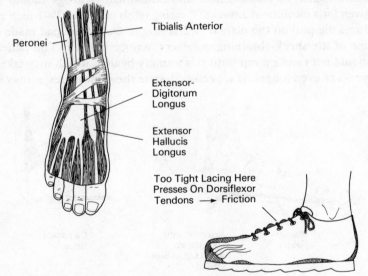

Fig. 6.3. Effect on dorsiflexor tendons of lacing shoes too tightly.

Peronei

Tibialis Anterior

Extensor-Digitorum Longus

Extensor Hallucis Longus

Too Tight Lacing Here Presses On Dorsiflexor Tendons → Friction

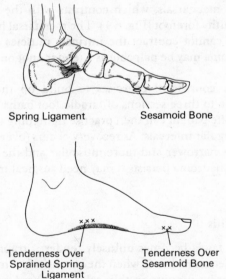

Spring Ligament

Sesamoid Bone

Tenderness Over Sprained Spring Ligament

Tenderness Over Sesamoid Bone

Fig. 6.4. Tenderness over the spring ligament and sesamoid bone.

LIGAMENTS

Spring ligament pain

The spring or calcaneo-navicular ligament may become sprained. This is particularly likely to happen in a pronated foot, in Morton's foot (short first metatarsal) and in a foot with poor intrinsic muscles. On standing, there is pain under the instep and tenderness of the spring ligament (see Fig. 6.4). Ice and ultrasound help relieve pain and inflammation, and measures to correct the basic problem should be taken, e.g. intrinsic foot muscles strengthened with exercise, pronation corrected with a medial heel wedge and float, and perhaps a medial arch support.

BURSAE

There is a subcutaneous bursa at the level of the insertion of the Achilles tendon into the calcaneum, which may be irritated and become swollen due to friction from a hard back to a shoe. This will settle if the shoe is altered and the area protected for a few days (see Fig. 6.5).

There is another bursa above the insertion of the Achilles tendon between the latter and the calcaneum. If there is a bony prominence here, this bursa may be trapped between bone and tendon, and become inflamed. This may not respond to conservative measures and the prominent bone may need to be removed to prevent recurrence.

BONES

Stress fractures of the metatarsal shaft

These may occur in runners or walkers. The second or third metatarsal is usually affected. Onset may be acute, or gradual and progressive. The foot is painful on standing and walking, relieved by sitting. There is swelling of the forefoot and localised tenderness over the metatarsal shaft. Palpable callus may be present after 2 weeks (see Fig. 6.6).

Treatment is rest from running or excessive walking for 4 weeks. It should become pain-free after 3 weeks' rest. Wearing a shoe with a stiff sole will stop the bone ends moving and decrease pain on walking. Strapping is not necessary.

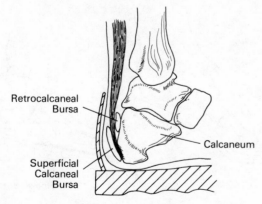

Fig. 6.5. Position of bursae in heel of foot.

Retrocalcaneal Bursa

Calcaneum

Superficial Calcaneal Bursa

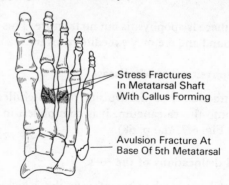

Fig. 6.6. Fractures of the metatarsals.

Stress Fractures In Metatarsal Shaft With Callus Forming

Avulsion Fracture At Base Of 5th Metatarsal

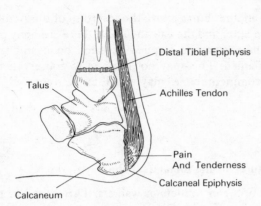

Fig. 6.7. Calcaneal apophysitis in the ankle of a 10 year old child.

Avulsion fracture of the base of the fifth metatarsal

The intermittent traction by the insertion of the tendon of peroneus brevis into the base of the fifth metatarsal may cause avulsion of the bone (see Fig. 6.6). It is not displaced, but a crack is seen on X-ray. This takes 4 weeks to heal and running should be abandoned during this time. Sometimes strapping may make it more comfortable, but is not essential.

Sometimes there is apophysitis but no fracture. This also responds to rest. Ultrasound and ice may expedite recovery.

Calcaneal apophysitis (Sever's disease)

This is due to traction or partial avulsion of the Achilles tendon from the insertion into the calcaneum. It is commonest in children and teenagers (see Fig. 6.7, and p. 68).

Fractures and dislocations of the toes

This is liable to happen when something solid is kicked by mistake, particularly if the individual is barefoot. Any deformity should be reduced and the toe splinted by taping it to its neighbour. Following a dislocation, the joint may fuse. As long as the toe is straight, this causes no problems.

Hallux rigidus

Recurrent or prolonged hyperextension of the hallux may sprain the joint capsule and cause inflammation and swelling with pain on movement, especially dorsiflexion. This makes 'push-off' in walking and running very painful. It usually recovers with prolonged rest. The best way to achieve this is to put a metal sole plate under the hallux and first metatarsal, and fit a rocker bar on the sole — the foot then rocks on this, rather than hyperextending the first metatarsophalangeal joint. It usually needs to be worn for 3–6 months (see Fig. 6.8). Occasionally osteoarthritic changes visible on X-ray develop in this joint. Operative treatment is usually by Keller's operation, which removes the metatarsal head — this relieves the pain but makes running impossible. A keen athlete may prefer to wear a rocker bar permanently.

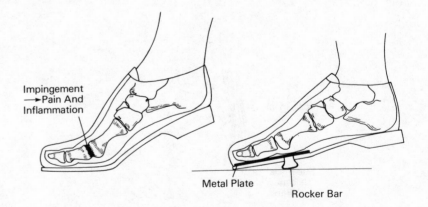

Fig. 6.8. Use of metal plate and rocker bar in hallux rigidus.

Hallux valgus

In this condition the first metatarsal is in varus position and the hallux is pulled back into valgus position by the pull of the tendons which are slightly malaligned due to the abnormal position of the metatarsal. A bunion (bursa) usually develops medially where the shoe rubs. Severe degrees of hallux valgus are not compatible with running sports. Minor degrees may be helped on a temporary basis by firm taping of the varus metatarsal, pulling the distal end in to the forefoot. As with hallux rigidus, operative treatment improves function for walking but does not allow running.

Osteochondritis of the tarsal navicular (Köehler's disease) head of metatarsal (Freiberg's disease)

There is pain and tenderness over the affected bone. X-rays may show nothing in early stages, but later the bone becomes dense and collapsed. Later it may re-expand.

It occurs in childhood and adolescence, particularly in the physically active. Trauma is thought to cause ischaemia of the growing bone, causing necrosis and collapse. Later regeneration and re-expansion of the bone may occur.

Rest from over-activity is usually enough to relieve pain and allow resolution. Rarely is it necessary to wear a plaster. Recovery may take up to 6 months.

7

The Ankle

...an overuse injury. The Achilles tendon has no synovial sheath, but runs through loose connective tissue which may become inflamed. Precipitating factors may be changing to very low-heeled shoes which increases the stretch on the tendon; wearing training shoes with stiff soles on some of the new synthetic surfaces which may have excessive recoil, or excessive running, particularly uphill. It is commoner in people with structural abnormalities of feet or knees. The tendon itself is not thickened, but the connective tissue around is, and there may be crepitus. It is frequently bilateral (see Fig. 7.1). Treatment consists of rest from running, physiotherapy with ice, ultrasound and stretching exercises and identification of the precipitating factors so that measures can be taken to prevent it recurring. Local peritendinous injections of hydrocortisone and local anaesthetic may hasten recovery.

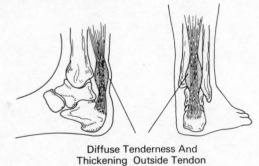

Diffuse Tenderness And
Thickening Outside Tendon

Fig. 7.1. Achilles peritendinitis.

Achilles tendinitis

This may be due to the top of a boot or a high tab on the back of a shoe impinging on the Achilles tendon when the foot is put into plantar flexion. It may also be due to a partial tear in the tendon which may be caused acutely by forced dorsiflexion of the foot. Long distance running, especially on hard surfaces, also causes it. The tendon develops a fusiform thickening which is tender (see Fig. 7.2). Dorsiflexion of the foot causes pain. Recovery usually takes at least 6 weeks, and is aided by ice and ultrasound. The tendon should be relaxed by wearing heeled shoes, and then once the tenderness has subsided, graded stretching should be done, progressing slowly. If the tendon is very inflamed, it may be advisable to immobilise the ankle in plaster in slight plantar flexion and to use crutches.

There is a danger of it becoming a recurrent problem. In middle-aged and elderly people, the tendon may develop cystic degeneration, which may or may not follow previous attacks. The cyst expands and the tendon thins around it. Such a cyst is often symptom-free, but there may be pain in the tendon. As there is considerable danger of sudden rupture, either partial or complete, it should be treated by operation. The tendon is opened, the cyst scooped out, and the tendon sewn up Postoperatively the ankle is put in plaster in equinus position for 6 weeks, and then very slowly mobilised at first on high heels, progressing with gradual stretching to lower heels.

Achilles' tendon rupture

Achilles' tendon rupture may be partial or complete. The defect may fill with haematoma, giving an appearance of continuity. The

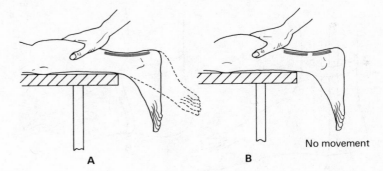

No movement

Fig. 7.3. Squeeze test for tears of Achilles tendon. A. Partial rupture. B. Total rupture.

A ruptured tendon will heal if it is immobilised with the ends in apposition for 6 weeks, followed by slow rehabilitation as described above. However, in many cases it is felt advisable to operate and suture the tendon, which is then rehabilitated as above, following 6 weeks in equinus plaster.

Partial ruptures are usually treated conservatively.

LIGAMENTS

Ankle sprains

INVERSION SPRAIN

This is a common injury due to an acute inversion of the ankle tearing the anterior talo-fibular and calcaneo-fibular components of the lateral collateral ligament. The tears are usually partial, but torn blood vessels may bleed copiously, causing a lot of swelling and bruising. There is tenderness over the ligaments and pain on stretching them. As long as the tears are partial, the ankle is stable. In young children, the tip of the fibula may be avulsed. This happens less frequently in adults, but if there is marked bony tenderness over

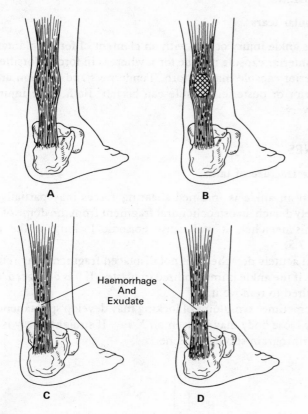

Haemorrhage
And
Exudate

Fig. 7.2. A. Achilles tendinitis. B. Degenerative cyst. C. Partial rupture. D. Total rupture.

squeeze test differentiates complete from partial rupture. The patient lies on a couch prone, with feet sticking beyond the end of the bed. The calf is squeezed and pushed up towards the knee just below the point of maximum diameter. If the tendon is intact, the foot will planta flex, but the foot will not move if the tendon is ruptured (see Fig. 7.3).

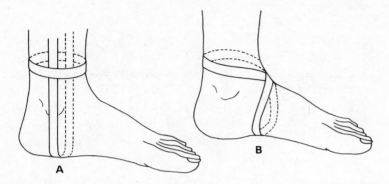

Fig. 7.4. Simple strapping of the ankle. A. T strap B. Figure of eight strap.

the lateral malleolus it should be X-rayed in case there is a fracture. Fractures and total ruptures should be referred for orthopaedic management.

Partial tears are treated actively with ice and ultrasound followed by graded exercises and early work on the wobbleboard to facilitate proprioception. A light compressive bandage is used. The patient is encouraged to walk as the rocking action keeps the ankle mobile and stimulates proprioceptive nerve endings. If the ankle is very painful, crutches and non-weight-bearing are allowed for 1–2 days. Recovery usually takes 2–3 weeks. When the player returns to sport, he may use a simple strapping as protection (see Fig. 7.4).

EVERSION SPRAIN

This happens less often and is usually caused by collision with another player or the ball. The deltoid ligament is very strong, so that frequently the medial malleolus fractures instead. For this reason, all medial ankle injuries should be X-rayed.

A partial ligament sprain is treated similarly to the lateral ligament sprain.

Capsular tears

If the ankle injury occurs with an element of forced plantar flexion, the anterior capsule may be torn, whereas in forced dorsiflexion, the posterior capsule may be torn. Tenderness and effusion around the anterior or posterior capsule can be felt. Both these injuries delay recovery.

BONES

Flake fracture of talus

When an ankle is sprained shearing forces may partially or completely detach an osteochondral fragment from the dome of the talus. If this detaches, it will cause episodic locking of the joint (see Fig. 7.5).

An acutely detached but not displaced fragment may reunite with bone if the ankle is immobilised in plaster. If it is displaced, surgery is required to remove it.

Sometimes symptoms of locking may develop spontaneously and a bony loose body may be seen on X-ray. If straight X-ray is negative, an arthrogram should be done.

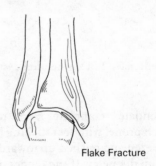

Flake Fracture

Fig. 7.5. Flake fracture of the talus.

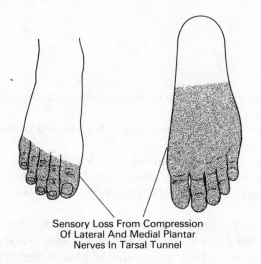

Sensory Loss From Compression
Of Lateral And Medial Plantar
Nerves In Tarsal Tunnel

Fig. 7.6. Posterior tibial neuritis.

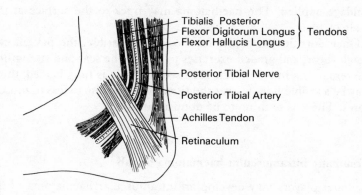

Tibialis Posterior
Flexor Digitorum Longus } Tendons
Flexor Hallucis Longus

Posterior Tibial Nerve

Posterior Tibial Artery

Achilles Tendon

Retinaculum

Fig. 7.7. Tarsal tunnel.

Sever's disease

This is an apophysitis of the calcaneum at the insertion of the Achilles tendon occurring in childhood and adolescence. It causes pain and swelling of the Achilles insertion. Symptoms settle with rest. Wearing shoes with a definite heel reduces traction on the tendon insertion. Sometimes excess bone is formed at the site of traction which causes problems in later life with the fit of shoes. If this is a nuisance it can be trimmed surgically (see Fig. 6.7, and p. 58).

NERVES

Posterior tibial neuritis

Trauma to the area just below the medial malleolus may cause entrapment of the posterior tibial nerve in the tarsal tunnel, with pain, tingling and numbness of the foot, together with weakness of the intrinsic muscles (see Figs 7.6 and 7.7). It usually settles spontaneously as the swelling goes down, but if it does not, the tarsal tunnel should be infiltrated with 50 mg hydrocortisone and local anaesthetic.

8
The Leg

SKIN LESIONS

Cuts, grazes and bruises to the shins are common. The skin is stretched tightly over the underlying bones, which means the blood supply is restricted and healing may be slow. Also there is little room for swelling so haematomas become tense and painful.

MUSCLE

Gastrocnemius muscle tear

This is a common injury in middle-aged people with a typical onset. It occurs when the person breaks into a sprint, e.g. at squash or tennis. There is a sensation of something snapping in the calf which may produce an audible crack, or the victim may be convinced that a blow came from the opponent. The calf swells and it may be too painful to weight-bear. Muscles fibres in the gastrocnemius, usually the medial head, tear near their insertion into the Achilles tendon. It used to be thought this syndrome was due to a ruptured plantaris muscle. A mild tear will cause some local tenderness and a limp. A grosser tear may be accompanied by considerable haemorrhage, resulting in intramuscular haematoma, which distends the flexor muscle compartment. The calf is hard and tender to palpation, and the tension prevents the foot dorsiflexing. This painful swollen calf may be mistaken for a deep vein thrombosis, and indeed a deep vein thrombosis does sometimes develop as a complication. At about 10 days after the injury, there is a risk of further bleeding, as at this stage the newly forming scar tissue is highly vascular, but has virtually no strength — an unguarded movement may tear it and cause a further haemorrhage.

The differential diagnosis is from a deep vein thrombosis of the calf and a ruptured Baker's cyst.

Treatment of the mild strain involves ice and ultrasound and a lot of stretching exercises. The patient should be taught a thorough stretching regime to use regularly before playing to prevent the scar tearing.

The more severe cases with a lot of bleeding may take 6–12 weeks to recover. If the foot will not dorsiflex to 90°, weight-bearing should not be attempted, and the patient should have bedrest with the leg elevated. Analgesics are required for pain, crutches should be provided, and the patient should have daily physiotherapy; ice followed by ultrasound relieves the pain, and speeds dispersal of the haematoma. Gentle isometric exercises are used, and a support bandage applied. The haematoma may track to the surface at the ankle or foot.

Once dorsiflexion of the foot to 90° is possible, the patient can weight-bear, and graded exercises to stretch the scar and strengthen the remaining intact muscle are used. When it is fully healed, there may be a visible hollow over the site of the tear due to loss of muscle fibres. There is nothing to be done about this.

Traumatic intramuscular haematoma of calf

Younger players may develop an intramuscular haematoma of the calf as a result of a direct blow from a boot or hockey-stick. Management is as above.

QUEEN ... CANCELL ... OF PHYSIOTHERA CENTR... HEALTH DISTRICT

Medial tibial soreness (shin splints)

Shin splints is a term used rather loosely to describe pain in the leg caused by running. Much has been written about the various compartment syndromes (see below). In the author's practice, these have been very rare, whereas medial tibial pain is seen very frequently. It appears to be an enthesopathy, the contractions of the soleus and gastrocnemius muscles in the superficial posterior compartment being transmitted by the fascia of the compartment to its insertion into the periosteum on the medial border of the tibia. The tugging pulls on the periosteum, raising it from the bone and causing inflammation. The symptoms are of pain in the shin which comes on with running, and goes off with stopping. It has gradually got more severe over the previous 1–2 weeks, until it makes the athlete pull up. Tenderness is limited to the medial tibial border usually in its middle/lower one-third and is often bilateral even though only one leg may be giving symptoms (see Fig. 8.1). There may be some local oedema.

Differential diagnosis is from stress fracture of the tibia (see below) and tenosynovitis of tibialis anterior.

In long-standing cases, there may be a sub-periosteal streak of new bone visible on X-ray. Bone scan shows a linear hot area along the border of the tibia quite different from the localised hot spot of a stress fracture.

The condition affects runners, especially if they are running on hard surfaces or have recently increased their mileage. It is particularly likely to occur in heavy people, so that large athletes such as rowers and rugby players, who are not the ideal build for running but are using running, often on roads, as part of their training, are frequently affected. Malalignment of the feet and legs is also a contributory factor.

Most cases respond to conservative treatment. Rest from running is essential for up to 2 weeks. Ice treatment is helpful and can be applied at home and used before and after a run when running is resumed. Ultrasound also reduces pain and inflammation. Non-steroidal anti-inflammatory tablets reduce the soreness.

Running should be restarted gradually. It is less likely to recur if running is done on smooth turf rather than on roads. Resilient footwear and shock-absorbing insoles are helpful. Suitable orthoses are occasionally helpful for people with pes cavus or pronated feet. The large athlete who is only running to achieve cardio-respiratory fitness would be advised to substitute cycling or swimming.

If the condition persists or recurs, symptoms may be relieved by surgery.

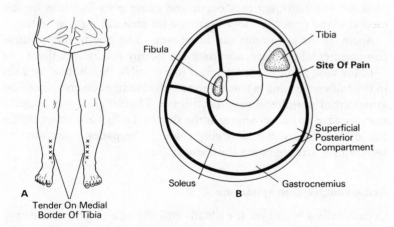

Fig. 8.1. Medial tibial pain (shin splints). A. Location of tenderness. B. Section through mid-calf.

Strained tibialis anterior

The tibialis anterior muscle can be strained by an unusual amount of running uphill or by using unaccustomedly flexible running shoes. This produces pain and tenderness over the belly of the tibialis anterior muscle just lateral to the upper part of the tibia, and pain in this position on resisted dorsiflexion of the ankle.

This is a typical muscle strain, and recovers spontaneously over a few days with avoidance of the precipitating cause, ice and stretching, and gradual return to training.

Anterior compartment syndrome

A different syndrome occurs in very long distance runners (e.g. marathon and supermarathon). In this case, the engorgement and swelling of the muscle caused by prolonged exertion is contained by the inelastic fascial compartment (see Fig. 8.2) and the pressure inside the compartment rises. This has been demonstrated with needle manometers. Above a critical level this impairs blood flow into the muscle, which develops ischaemic pain, forcing the runner to stop. It slowly subsides after this, behaving very much like the pain of intermittent claudication being also due to muscle ischaemia. In

compartment syndrome the arterial pulses are usually retained, the smaller intramuscular arterioles and capillaries probably being the vessels which collapse. The nerves passing through the anterior compartment may also suffer ischaemia, and cause numbness of the foot as part of the syndrome. At rest there are no physical signs except that the muscles are bulky.

This compression syndrome is not common. It can be treated successfully by extensive fasciotomy, but this should only be done after needle manometry has confirmed an excessive rise in intra-compartmental pressure on exercise.

Posterior compartment syndrome

Similar ischaemic pain occurs due to swelling of the muscles in the superficial and deep posterior compartments on prolonged exercise. Engorgement of gastrocnemius and soleus causes pain in the calf. Engorgement of the posterior tibialis and other muscles in the deep posterior compartment may occur and cause pain that may be felt medial to the tibia. As above there are no physical signs at rest.

Again, if the symptoms can be proven to be due to raised intra-compartmental pressure, adequate fasciotomy will relieve them.

In the case of older runners, it is just possible that ischaemic pain in the calf on running is true intermittent claudication and is the first symptom of peripheral vascular disease. Thermography is a useful non-invasive way of screening as the skin in the foot and lower leg on the affected side is demonstrably colder. The patients can then be referred for arteriography if necessary.

Acute compression syndrome

Occasionally a blow over the tibialis anterior or a tibial fracture may produce enough bleeding to raise the pressure in the compartment, and cause prolonged ischaemia of the nerve, and collapse of the anterior tibial artery with loss of the dorsalis pedis pulse. This rare

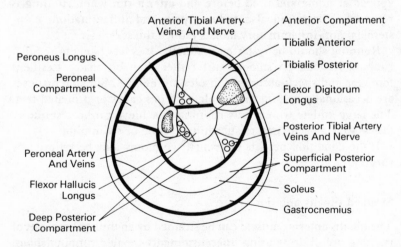

Fig. 8.2. Fascial compartments of the leg.

Anterior Tibial Artery
Veins And Nerve

Anterior Compartment

Tibialis Anterior

Tibialis Posterior

Flexor Digitorum
Longus

Peroneus Longus

Peroneal
Compartment

Posterior Tibial Artery
Veins And Nerve

Peroneal Artery
And Veins

Flexor Hallucis
Longus

Superficial Posterior
Compartment

Deep Posterior
Compartment

Soleus

Gastrocnemius

occurrence is an emergency requiring immediate surgery to open the compartment and relieve the pressure. If this is not done irreversible ischaemia and compression occur, and amputation may be required.

NERVES

Neuronopraxia of common peroneal nerve

The common peroneal nerve lies subcutaneously as it winds around the fibula just below its head. A kick or blow in this region may cause transient or more long-standing loss of transmission in the nerve. The immediate blow will produce an instantaneous electric shock-like sensation down the cutaneous distribution of the nerve to the anterior shin and dorsum of foot and toes (Fig. 8.3), followed by

Fig. 8.3. Sensory loss from lesion of common peroneal nerve.

numbness with paralysis of peroneal muscles and dorsiflexion of the foot. This recovers spontaneously in a few minutes.

With neuronopraxia or neuronotmesis, the sensory and motor changes last longer and the patient walks with a foot drop.

Recovery is certain, though it may take many weeks. An electromyogram may be useful in predicting length of recovery. In the early stage an ortholene back splint worn inside the shoe to keep the foot at 90° will prevent tripping. As soon as there is a flicker of muscle function, a programme of active exercises should be used to strengthen the re-innervated muscle.

Nerve root irritation

Pain and tingling on the lateral side of the leg, possible extending into the dorsum of the foot and toes, may be due to irritation of nerve roots in the low lumbar spine (see Fig. 8.4). In this case, there will be no local cause for the symptoms. If the symptoms are bilateral, this is even more suggestive.

The patient should be asked about backache now or in the past, and a careful examination of the lumbar spine should be made. These symptoms are frequently due to a prolapsed disc at L5/S1 irritating nerve roots. It may occur occasionally in the absence of backache as a symptom, though there are usually physical signs on examination.

Compression syndromes

As mentioned above, the compression syndromes may cause ischaemia of the peripheral nerves contained in the fascial compartments, e.g. musculocutaneous and anterior tibial nerves in the anterior compartment, and posterior tibial nerves in the deep posterior compartment. The symptoms of nerve palsy wear off soon after running stops.

BONES

Stress fractures

Stress fractures of both fibula and tibia occur as a result of running. Typical sites are about 5 cm (2 inches) above the top of the lateral malleolus on the fibula, and in the top third of the tibial shaft. These two points lie at the bottom and top of the extent of the interosseous membrane, which tethers the bones to each other — below and above they may spring more and more freely as the bones spring with each footfall, and the junction between a relatively fixed and a more mobile zone produces mechanical stress. However, stress fractures occur at other levels too. They may be bilateral.

Symptoms may be of sudden onset, but more frequently have come on gradually and progressively, occurring more severely and earlier, until finally becoming too painful to run at all.

Once the diagnosis is established by X-ray, bone scan or thermography, the athlete should avoid running altogether, and limit walking to short distances. The recommended rest periods are 6 weeks for fibula and 8–10 weeks for tibia. Immobilisation with plaster of Paris is not usually necessary.

The differential diagnosis is from medial skin soreness (shin splints), pathological fracture in a tumour and subperiosteal haematoma following a blow.

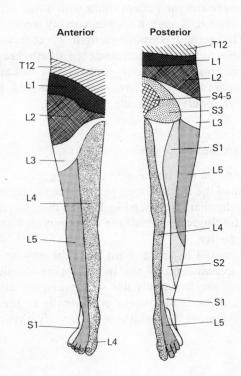

Fig. 8.4. Dermatomes of the leg.

9
The Knee Joint

The knee is the anatomical region most frequently injured at sport — 26% in our series of injuries. It is susceptible to acute trauma in contact sports, and to a variety of overuse syndromes from running. It should be remembered that pain may be referred from the hip to the anterior knee, especially but not exclusively in children. When assessing a knee injury an accurate history is especially helpful.

THE PATELLA

Haematoma

The patella may be bruised by kicks or by falling onto a hard surface. This may cause a haemorrhagic effusion into the prepatellar bursa or even the knee joint itself. There may be extensive bruising subcutaneously. The patella may also have been jammed hard against the lower end of the femur, causing symptoms of patello-femoral irritation (see below).

History and examination confirm the diagnosis. Ice treatment with quadriceps exercises, initially static but progressing to active after the soreness has diminished, resolve the problem. If the prepatellar bursa is swollen, this can be aspirated and dressed with a firm pad and bandage to try to prevent recurrence.

Patello-femoral syndrome

In this condition there is inflammation of the soft tissue underlying the cartilage on the back of the patella (see Fig. 9.1). Compression of this tissue against the femur as the quadriceps contract to extend the knee causes of symptoms pain and stiffness on running. In the early stages it may be possible to run through it, pain and stiffness returning on resting after the run. Other activities in which the knee is extended cause pain, such as walking downhill or downstairs. It is also typical that the knee becomes stiff and uncomfortable when sitting still with the knee flexed, e.g. in a car, or at the cinema. The patient may notice the knee-cap creaking. Often symptoms are bilateral, or the symptoms may be unilateral and the signs bilateral.

The syndrome is due to excessive friction between the back of the patella and the lower end of the femur, which may be due to overuse. It is certainly a common problem where there is malalignment and in girls who have a greater Q-angle related to the wider pelvis (see Fig. 9.2). Imbalance of the quadriceps when the vastus medialis is relatively weak is another underlying factor as the other quadriceps muscles tend to pull the patella laterally, increasing patello-femoral friction. It is a common problem during and just after the adolescent growth spurt, apparently related to muscle inco-ordination and imbalance. It is common in 18–22 year olds who are doing a lot of sport, due to straight overuse, or to muscle imbalance. This may develop as a result of training as many of the training schedules involve resisted exercises with the knees in partial flexion, and the vastus medialis is not strengthened under these circumstances as it only acts during the final 5–10° of knee extension.

It also afflicts middle-aged people, relatively sedentary most of the year, who go mountain walking on holiday; the steep descents causing patello-femoral irritation in those who have not done their static quads exercises beforehand, and hence have relatively weak vastus medialis muscles.

There may be nothing to see, though if symptoms are acute, there may be slight swelling visible around the patella. The vastus medialis

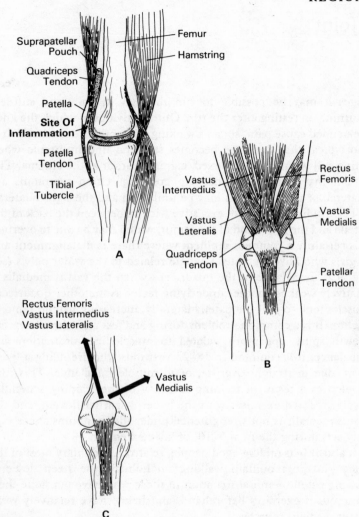

Fig. 9.1. The knee joint. A Patello-femoral syndrome. B. Muscles of the knee joint C. Lines of pull of the muscles.

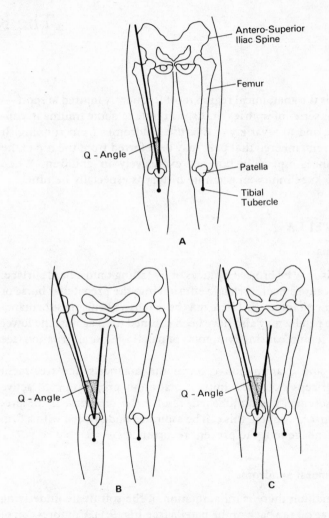

Fig. 9.2. The Q-angles in various malalignments. A. Normal Q-angle. B. Wide pelvis with increased Q-angle. C. Femoral torsion and genu valgum.

may be wasted, or small compared to the muscle mass of the other quads. The alignment of the legs should be checked, looking for increased Q-angle which may be due to a broad pelvis, a lateral placement of the tibial tubercle, or abnormalities of the patella such as patella alta. Clark's test is positive — holding the patella against the femur whilst the patient contracts the quadriceps causes crepitus, pain and inability to hold the contraction. Examination of the tibio-femoral joint is normal.

Treatment consists of rest, NSAIDs and physiotherapy. Ice deceases the soreness and allows initially static quads exercises. These can be stepped up to active and resisted exercises in near extension which will selectively strengthen the vastus medialis. If the vastus medialis does not build up with active and resisted exercise, faradism may be used to give a helpful boost. Once the soreness has subsided and the muscle is improving, running can then be restarted gradually. The cure rate is high, but symptoms may recur if the vastus medialis is allowed to weaken. The exercises should be kept up regularly. If symptoms persist, the patient should be referred to an orthopaedic surgeon for consideration of a lateral retinaculum release or tibial tubercle transplant if appropriate.

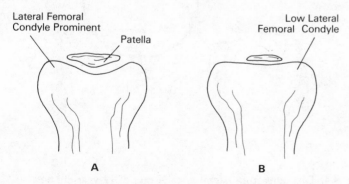

Fig. 9.3. Patella. A. Skyline view of normal patella. B. patella alta.

Chondromalacia patellae

This may follow from long-standing patello-femoral irritation. cartilage on the back of the patella becomes roughened and erode Crepitus and pain are the symptoms. X-ray views may show bony sclerosis or erosion of the back of the patella. The diagnosis can be confirmed at arthroscopy. Treatment is difficult: it may be relieved by NSAIDs and physiotherapy, and sometimes patellectomy is indicated, though this is a desperate measure, as having no patella to protect the front of the knee joint is a considerable disadvantage.

Dislocation of the patella

The normal patella is difficult to dislocate, as it is held in its position in the groove at the end of the femur by the medial and lateral retinacula. (see Fig. 9.3). The angle of pull of the quadriceps tends to displace the patella laterally, but slip is prevented by impingement on the high lateral wall of the patella groove, and by the medial pull of the vastus medialis, especially nearing full extension.

If the patella is given a hard thrust laterally, as the knee is nearing extension, the patella may jump out of the groove, dislocating laterally and tearing the medial retinaculum. It takes a major force to do this the first time, but subsequently it may dislocate easily. It usually reduces spontaneously. A bloody effusion often develops post-traumatically. The apprehension test is diagnostic — the patient gets very uneasy if the patella is pushed firmly sideways.

The patella may dislocate spontaneously if it is abnormal. Patella alta is a small patella placed higher than usual, and often associated with a low lateral lip to the femoral patella groove. Tightness of the lateral retinaculum is another cause.

It may be possible to control dislocation by wearing a special patella support knee splint. However, if recurrent dislocation continues, surgery may be required. A lateral release may cure it.

of trauma, e.g. a kick or kneeling on a
...asionally it occurs as an overuse injury in
...endon itself is tender, with a little diffuse
...ound, ice and frictions usually heal it.
...cortisone and local anaesthetic should be
...on.

Partial avulsion of lower pole of the patella
(Sinding–Larsen–Johnson syndrome)

Repetitive pulling on the patellar tendon in the lower pole of the
patella may cause an apophysitis or partial avulsion of the patellar
tendon. There is usually some swelling and tenderness localised to
the lower pole of patella. It is particularly common on the take-off leg
of hurdlers and high jumpers.

Osgood–Schlatter disease

This condition causes pain and swelling in the region of the tibial
tubercle, and is an overuse injury afflicting 10–16 year olds. It often
comes on during or just after a growth spurt. It is due to repetitive
and forced knee extension damaging the epiphysis of the tibial
tubercle. Initially there is just inflammation, but if overuse continues, the tibial tubercle may become fragmented. As ossification
proceeds, a large and more prominent tibial tubercle forms on the affected side. It is commonly caused by football in which case it usually
affects the dominant kicking leg. In basketball players or runners, it is
usually bilateral.

Diagnosis depends on the age and typical history. There is a
localised tender bump over the tibial tubercle. If symptoms have
been present for some weeks or if the swelling is very pronounced,
the tibial tubercle should be X-rayed. This will show if there is
disruption of the tibial tubercle (see Fig. 9.4). Very occasionally a
flake of bone may interfere with the action of the patellar tendon,
and require removal.

Symptoms usually settle with rest from all activity except moderate
walking and non-competitive swimming and cycling. Ice treatment
is also helpful. If these measures do not relieve symptoms in 3 weeks
(and this is usually because the child does not rest enough), the knee
should be put in a plaster of Paris extension cylinder for a minimum
of 3 weeks — up to 6 weeks may be required. When the knee has
been pain-free for a week, the plaster can be removed and a gradual
return to sport allowed. The child and parents should be cautioned
about overdoing sport, and warned that the condition is liable to
recur if the knee is abused, until such time as the epiphysis fuses —
usually between ages 16 and 18.

There are usually no long-term sequelae, apart from a prominent
tibial tubercle. Occasionally a residual flake of bone may give symptoms and need removing.

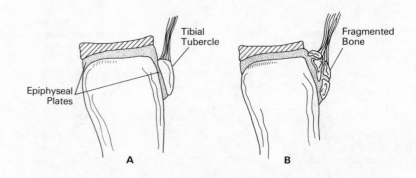

Fig. 9.4. Diagrams from lateral knee X-rays of 12-year old boys.
A. Normal. B. Fragmented tibial tubercle.

MEDIAL SIDE OF KNEE

Sprained medial ligament

The medial ligament is taut throughout the range of normal knee movements, different fibres being tensed in different degrees of flexion. The ligament resists external rotation of the tibia, and valgus forces, hence it is these movements, especially when applied forcefully, which damage the medial ligament. It is a common injury in contact sports when the combination of a tackle applying a rotatory force to the knee, whilst the boot is stuck into the surface of the pitch, produces marked stress on the ligament. Tackles or falls in which the knee is forced into valgus position also damage the medial ligament. In the majority of cases the tear is only partial — if the ligament is totally ruptured the knee becomes unstable.

The history is usually very suggestive. There may be swelling around the medial aspect of the knee, or an effusion. There is local tenderness on the line of the ligament — usually at the joint line, but it may extend down to the insertion into the tibia 7.5–10 cm (3–4 inch) below the joint line. The valgus stress test will cause discomfort and the degree of 'give' will increase with greater degrees of stretching or tearing of the ligament. If there is appreciable give with the knee in full extension, this suggests the anterior cruciate ligament is damaged, in addition to the medial ligament. If the knee is unstable, the patient should be referred to an orthopaedic surgeon, who may operate or treat it conservatively in a plaster cylinder.

If the knee is stable, this implies only a partial tear, and active treatment is best. Local ice and ultrasound are used daily, together with an active exercise programme to build up the quadriceps and hamstrings. Recovery usually takes about 3 weeks and the patient should be watched closely throughout. The deeper layers of the medial ligament are attached to the edge of the medial meniscus — sometimes this is torn at the time of injury, but is undetected at initial presentation. Such a tear will become apparent during the treatment and cause locking as exercise and loading of the knee is increased. It is wise to regard the physiotherapy as a prolonged trial for damage to internal knee structures as well as a treatment. NSAIDs are helpful if there is significant inflammation.

Breast-stroke knee

This is a chronic sprain of the medial ligament, often bilateral, caused by a wide kick in breast-stroke giving repeated valgus stress. Recognition that this was an overuse injury led to modification of the stroke, so that the breast-stroke kick is now much narrower — the injury has become rare.

Pellegrini–Stieda disease

This condition is pain and tenderness over the medial ligament associated with calcification and sometimes ossification in the ligament. It was originally described in cavalry officers, where the prolonged valgus riding position and continual friction against the saddle produced microtrauma, and led to heterotopic calcification visible on X-ray. It is sometimes seen in other sports following repeated medial ligament sprains, or haematomas from direct blows. The pain and tenderness usually settle with ice and ultrasound, but if this fails, a hydrocortisone injection may be effective. Only very occasionally is surgery required to remove a flake of calcium or bone.

LATERAL SIDE OF KNEE

Ilio-tibial tract friction, or 'snapping band'

The thick fascia lata on the lateral side of the thigh extends as the ilio-tibial band across the knee joint and is inserted into the tibia. The point of insertion lies anterior to the knee axis in extension, and posterior to it in flexion, so that with each step the band moves backwards and forwards across the axis of the knee (see Fig. 9.5). Running long distances may cause friction, so that the ilio-tibial tract

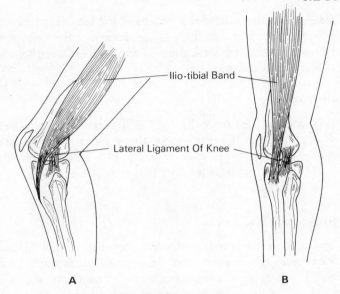

Ilio-tibial Band

Lateral Ligament Of Knee

A   B

Fig. 9.5. Movement of ilio-tibial band relative to lateral femoral condyle. A. Flexion. B. Extension.

becomes swollen and thickened; running becomes increasingly painful and the thickened band may actually give a snapping sensation as it crosses the joint axis. This problem is more likely to occur when there is a varus force on the knee, e.g. in individuals with bandy legs, or running long distances on a camber, or in long distance cyclists when the set of the pedals is wrong.

On examination, tenderness is over the ilio-tibial tract and not the lateral ligament or biceps tendon. It is helpful to examine the knee in extension and flexed to 90°, to help separate these structures. The tract may be thickened and feel cord-like. Sometimes recurrent snap can be felt by palpating gently with the knee flexed and extended.

If the athlete has not run for a few days, however, there may be no physical signs. The history should be suggestive, but the diagnosis can only be confirmed by sending the individual off to run until symptoms recur and then examining the knee 'hot from the track'.

Treatment consists of ice and ultrasound to reduce swelling and local inflammation. NSAIDs are useful. Measures must then be taken to avoid recurrence. The application of ice before and after a run is helpful, but changes in technique and practice may be of more long-term benefit. For instance, running on the same side of a cambered road should be avoided — if there is no suitable flat surface for running, the problem can be avoided by changing the side of the road every half mile or so. The legs and feet should be inspected carefully for malalignment, e.g. equinovarus or equinovalgus — a build-up on the outside of the shoe, or an orthosis inside the shoe may correct the problem.

Sprained lateral ligament

The lateral collateral ligament of the knee is stressed by varus forces and by forced internal rotation of the tibia. It is a common injury in contact sports, the forces producing injury being opposite to those damaging the medial ligament.

Again, the history is suggestive. There may be local swelling, but as the lateral ligament lies outside the capsule effusion is unusual with a lateral ligament tear. The ligament is tender — it can be made to stand out by pulling the knee into the tailor or lotus position. Varus stress causes pain and shows up ligamentous laxity. As with the medial ligament, total rupture with instability should be referred to an orthopaedic surgeon. Partial tears are treated with intensive physiotherapy.

Popliteus sprain and tendinitis

The popliteus muscle prevents the femur from sliding forward on the tibial plateau (see Fig. 9.6). It is particularly stressed by running

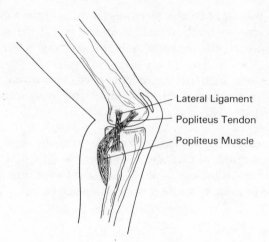

Fig. 9.6. Diagram showing popliteus tendon and muscle.

downhill. Pain and tenderness may be felt posteriorly in the popliteal fossa over the belly of the muscle, or laterally where the tendon runs below the lateral collateral ligament and inserts into the edge of the lateral femoral condyle — there may be tenderness over the tendon just anterior to the lateral ligament.

Symptoms settle with physiotherapy. Running on hills should be avoided till recovery is complete.

Superior tibio-fibular joint sprain

This joint may rarely be sprained or even disrupted by a forceful blow displacing the head of the fibula posteriorly. Minor degrees recover with physiotherapy and time. If totally disrupted, it may continue to give symptoms of pain and it may be necessary to remove the fibular head and re-implant the lateral collateral ligament and tendon of biceps.

INTERNAL DERANGEMENT OF THE KNEE

This is a useful term which includes damage to the bony joint surfaces and articular cartilage, cruciate ligaments and menisci (see Fig. 9.7). It recognises the fact that it is exceedingly difficult to make an accurate diagnosis on clinical grounds of mischief inside the knee joint. It also implies the necessity for referral to an orthopaedic surgeon. Plain X-rays should always be done. In some centres surgeons now proceed staight to arthroscopy rather than ask for arthrography with single or double contrast.

The main symptoms of internal damage of the knee are locking, giving-way and effusion.

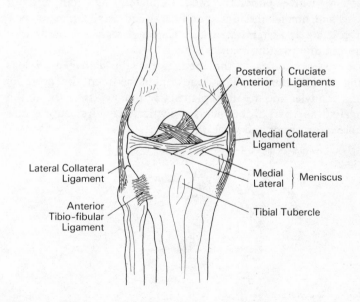

Fig. 9.7. Anterior view of knee joint with the patella removed.

Locking

Locking is due to a loose body getting trapped betwen joint surfaces, causing momentary or prolonged mechanical jamming. It may be due to the following.

Torn meniscus: This is usually caused by a twisting force on the weight-bearing knee causing a femoral condyle to shear the fibrocartilage of the meniscus — usually along the thin inside edge. It is particularly likely to happen when a rotatory force tears the collateral ligament, allowing further anterior movement of the femoral condyle on the tibia as it twists, tearing the cruciate ligament and grinding and splitting the meniscus. This injury was named by O'Donoghue as the 'Unhappy Triad'. Depending on the direction of rotation it involves either the medial collateral ligament, anterior cruciate and medial meniscus, or lateral collateral ligament, posterior cruciate and lateral meniscus. Cartilage tears also occur with less devastating twisting injuries.

The posterior poles of the menisci may be damaged by load bearing in full flexion. This traps them between the posterior femoral condyles and the tibial plateau, and may cause a tear in this relatively flimsy part of the menisci. Typical activities causing such tears are deep squats and squat thrusts.

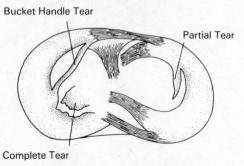

Fig. 9.8. Diagram to show the torn menisci of the knee.

The tears may be complete, detaching a portion of fibrocartilage altogether, or partial, so that the loose part is tethered at one end to the meniscus, or a bucket handle tear (see Fig. 9.8).

Degenerative cyst: In the middle-aged a degerative cyst in the meniscus may give rise to discomfort and intermittent locking (see Fig. 9.9).

Bone and cartilage loose bodies: An endochondral fracture may detach a chunk of cartilage or cartilage and bone. If the former, it will not be visible on X-ray. If diagnosed soon after detachment, it may be possible to staple it back into place (see Fig. 9.9).

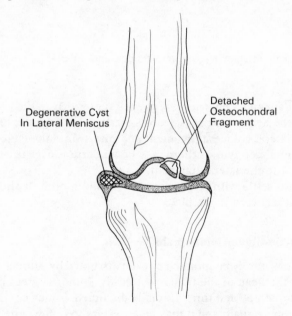

Fig. 9.9. Diagram to show degenerative cyst and detached bone fragments in knee.

Osteochondritis dissecans is a condition with one or more loose osteochondral fragments. They probably detach during adolescence, but may not give symptoms until later. The cartilage will grow because its cells receive adequate nourishment from the synovial fluid — small fragments will begin to cause locking as they grow bigger. The usual site of detachment is from the lateral aspect of the medial femoral condyle, possibly due to impingement of the posterior tibial spine.

When the cruciate ligaments are stressed, they may avulse a piece of bone from the tibial attachment, and this may cause locking.

Giving-way

This is due to laxity or rupture of the cruciate ligaments and is aggravated by laxity of the collateral ligaments. The cruciate ligaments resist anterior–posterior movement of the femur on the tibia.

The anterior cruciate ligament resists backward movement of the femur on the tibia. If lax or ruptured, the tibia can be drawn forward (the Anterior Drawer sign and Lachman's sign)(no relation to the author!). The anterior cruciate ligament lies posterior to the joint cavity, but its anterior aspect projects into the joint space and is covered with synovium and a leash of blood vessels, which tend to tear when the ligament is damaged, causing a haemarthrosis.

The posterior cruciate resists forward movement of the femur on the tibia, and if lax or torn, the tibia can be pushed posteriorly unduly far (Posterior Drawer sign). Bleeding from a torn posterior cruciate ligament is seen in the popliteal fossa.

In the presence of an effusion, it is difficult to elicit the drawer signs, and also the fluid may force the joint surfaces apart, so that locking does not occur.

Effusion

It is wise to aspirate an effusion of any size for a variety of reasons. It is most easily done through the lateral aspect of the suprapatellar pouch, where there is no intervening muscle. If full aseptic precautions are taken, it can be done in the consulting room. The advantages are as follows:

• Determination of the nature of effusion: if the fluid is heavily blood-stained, this suggests either an endochondral fracture or a damaged anterior cruciate ligament.

Clear fluid may be due to traumatic synovitis, or an inflammatory exudate due to damage to the collateral ligaments or other neighbouring structures, or to bruising following a fall on a hard surface. Synovitis due to a rheumatological condition such as rheumatoid arthritis, ankylosing spondylitis or Reiter's syndrome, may occasionally be precipitated by sport and present at a Sports Injury Clinic. In this case, it may be bilateral or recurrent. Similarly, septic arthritis may first present symptoms after exercise. All aspirated fluid should be sent for culture.

• Diagnosis: removing a tense effusion allows the joint to be examined and tests for ligament laxity and stability carried out. If the knee is very painful, some local anaesthetic can be instilled first.

• Relief of symptoms: a tense effusion causes pain, muscle spasm and embarrasses movement. If it contains blood, the blood irritates the synovium causing pain and further effusion. Distension of the joint capsule is associated with rapid wasting of the muscles about the joint. Aspiration relieves discomfort and speeds the rate of recovery. It will take days for a bloody effusion to be absorbed spontaneously. Recurrence of the effusion may be reduced by ice treatment followed by a firm support with bandage or elasticated support. If necessary, it may be aspirated again.

Baker's cyst

An effusion may become trapped in the popliteal region, and by a valve-like action of a fold of synovium, the tension will rise, forming a tense prominent popliteal swelling known as a Baker's cyst (see Fig. 9.10). This may burrow or rupture into the gastrocnemius muscle causing symptoms and signs mimicking those of a deep vein thrombosis. Arthrography confirms the diagnosis by showing the leak into the tissue. Treatment consists of aspiration of the cyst and treatment of the cause of the effusion. Once it has ruptured, it will heal spontaneously, but fluid may re-accumulate.

BURSAE

There are approximately 15 bursae around the knee joint, the number varying between individuals. A few of these quite commonly become enlarged or inflamed by sport (see Fig. 9.11).

Prepatellar bursa

Falls where the patella hits a hard surface cause haemorrhage or traumatic effusion in the bursa, which may be recurrent. It produces an egg-shaped swelling on the front of the patella.

Superficial infrapatellar bursa

This may be irritated by kneeling upright on a rough or hard surface — 'Clergyman's knee'.

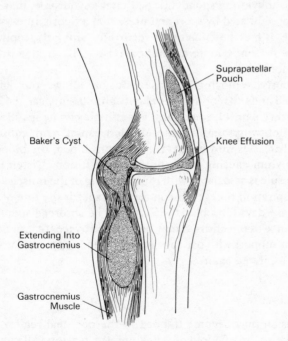

Fig. 9.10. Baker's cyst.

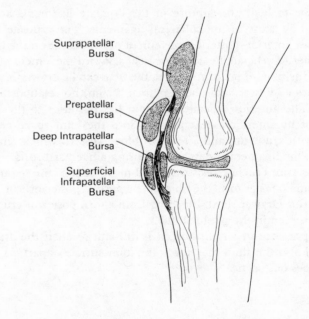

Fig. 9.11. Common sites of bursitis around the knee joint.

Deep infrapatellar bursa

This lies behind the lower patella tendon, and the tibia may be inflamed by repetitive forced knee extension, especially jumping.

Suprapatellar bursa

This is continuous with the main cavity of the knee joint, and is distended when there is a knee effusion. The lateral side of the bursa is subcutaneous, and is the easiest site to tap a knee effusion.

Treatment of bursitis

If the enlarged bursa is causing symptoms, it may be aspirated, and a firm support applied to discourage re-accumulation of fluid. If it recurs, an injection of hydrocortisone into the bursa may be effective.

MUSCLES

Muscle strains

QUADRICEPS

The rectus femoris is the part of the quadriceps which is strained most frequently. Activities such as rowing, kicking a football and weight-lifting stress the muscle. Usually the tear occurs mid-belly, causing diffuse tenderness and pain on resisted movement. Occasionally total rupture of the muscle may occur with a major force such as power lifts. If seen immediately, it may be possible to suture it. Once the ends have retracted, repair is impossible.

HAMSTRINGS

An acute hamstring tear usually occurs on sprinting, as the muscle is principally responsible for the power of a push-off. It is particularly likely to occur if the warm-up and stretching have been inadequate or neglected, and also in cold weather. The tear is usually in the belly of the muscle, with localised tenderness on palpation and pain on resisted movement (see Fig. 10.1). If neither of these is present, the lumbo-sacral region should be checked as pain from S1 root irritation is felt here.

Chronic strains may develop when an acute sprain is neglected or mishandled. A regular stretching regime is essential during recovery. If omitted, a contracted and puckered scar forms which tears again easily and repeatedly, so that eventually a palpable knot of tender scar tissue may form which severely restricts activity. The best treatment for this is to prevent it by treating acute tears with physiotherapy and allowing no competitive sport until the injury is adequately healed.

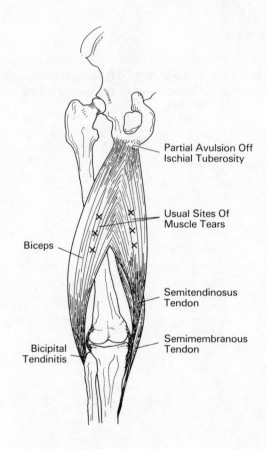

Fig. 10.1. Diagram of hamstrings showing common sites of injury.

Once a chronic tear has occurred, it may gradually be broken down by deep frictions. This is a painful but effective form of treatment, though complete recovery may take weeks or months. It should be combined with stretching, and adequate stretching and warm-up should be continued permanently.

AVULSION OF THE HAMSTRING

Occasionally the muscle insertion into the ischial tuberosity is torn, causing pain and tenderness right on the bone. This may take 3–4 months to heal, and all strenuous activity should be avoided during this time. Hamstring tendinitis may recur — usually of the biceps tendon.

ADDUCTOR STRAINS

These strains occur in the belly of adductor longus or adductor magnus, and are due to forced abduction or resisted adduction. It is a common football injury. Strains in the muscle belly recover quickly, as there is plenty of muscle to take the pull off the damaged fibres. Occasionally a major force may partially avulse the muscle off the pubic insertion. This injury, as with the hamstring avulsion, takes a long time to heal, and the muscle insertion must be protected from stress until it is fully healed — the time required is in the order of 3–4 months.

ILIO-PSOAS STRAINS

The ilio-psoas muscle is a powerful flexor of the hip joint. Injury is commonly referred to as a groin strain, because it is the muscular part of iliacus where it crosses the hip joint, which is most commonly torn. However, the muscle belly of psoas major extends up to its insertions into the transverse processes of the lumbar vertebra. A strain of this part of the muscle may result in abdominal pain and tenderness on deep palpation at the back of the abdominal cavity.

Intramuscular haematoma of thigh

The dead leg, Charlie horse or cork thigh injury occurs in contact sports and is due to a direct blow to the thigh; usually from a knee or boot. The vastus lateralis or intermedius are most often involved — the blow to a muscle which has become vasodilated and engorged due to exercise and heat ruptures blood vessels, causing extravasation of up to 1–1.5 pints of blood into the muscle. The muscle inside the fascial compartment becomes distended and this impairs flexion of the knee. If the knee cannot be flexed to 90°, this implies haemorrhage of considerable size.

Recovery is slow, as the haemorrhage has to be broken down and resorbed. Attempts to aspirate the blood are not recommended, as it is not localised, but diffuse and clotted. If sport is resumed before the muscle has completely recovered, further haemorrhage may occur. This is a site prone to ectopic calcification, which may proceed to myositis ossificans (see Fig. 10.2). A bony spur forms, usually attached to the femur, and may interfere with quadriceps action. It seems this complication is commoner when the player resumes activity too soon. It is wise to use crutches and keep the patient non-weight-bearing until 90° knee flexion can be achieved, and then to proceed slowly with rehabilitation until there is a full range of knee movement and no local tenderness.

BURSAE

Trochanteric bursitis

The trochanteric bursae lie just proximal and distal to the greater trochanter below the gluteus medius and gluteus maximus. They may become inflamed by movement of gluteus medius tendon and gluteus maximus muscle, as an overuse injury, due to movement of the fibres of the gluteal muscles moving over the bursae and causing friction. It is commoner in women, probably because the pelvis is wide and the pull of the gluteal tendons is more across the bursae. It is also likely to occur due to malalignment of the legs, an adducted gait, or to running on a cambered surface. There is local tenderness around the greater trochanter, and pain on running or walking.

The acute symptoms resolve with 1–3 local injections of hydrocortisone, and local anaesthetic, but the precipitating cause should be sought and corrected where possible.

LIGAMENTS

Sprained hip

The capsular ligaments of the hip joint are very strong, and protected by the hip muscles.

A forced extension of the hip may sprain the anterior ilio-femoral ligament. This will cause flexor spasm of the hip, tenderness deep over the front of the acetabulum and pain on extension. Recovery may take 3–4 months. The structure is very deep, so short-wave diathermy is required to reach it. Hip strengthening and mobilising exercises should be used — hydrotherapy is good for this. NSAIDs are useful.

A normal hip is unlikely to be sprained other than by a major stress. However, if there is underlying osteoarthritis due to advanced age, or previous hip pathology, the change in bony surfaces may be associated with ligamentous laxity and the capsular ligament may sprain more easily. X-rays should be taken to look for a predisposing cause.

BONES

Slipped femoral epiphysis

In growing children the epiphysis may slip suddenly whilst playing sport, but often the slip is gradual and the child may report pain and limping over some weeks previously. Often the pain is felt in the knee. It occurs between the ages of 10 and 15, and although it may be

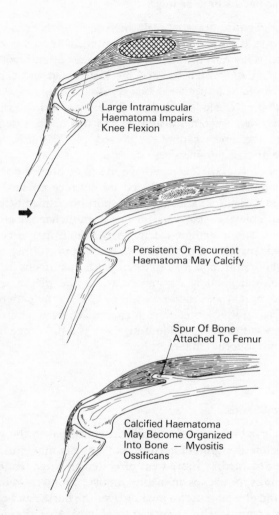

Large Intramuscular Haematoma Impairs Knee Flexion

Persistent Or Recurrent Haematoma May Calcify

Spur Of Bone Attached To Femur

Calcified Haematoma May Become Organized Into Bone — Myositis Ossificans

Fig. 10.2. Intramuscular haematoma of the thigh.

commoner in overweight children, it also occurs in those of normal build. Even though pain may be felt in the knee, there is no tenderness, and no restricted movement at this joint. However, hip movements are limited, and reproduce the pain. X-ray shows widening of the epiphysis and the degree of slip of the femoral head. The child should be referred to an orthopaedic surgeon for management.

Minor degrees of slip may be undetected in childhood, but cause early osteoarthritis in later life due to distortion of bone surfaces.

Perthes disease (Legg–Calvé–Perthes disease)

This condition is a form of osteochondritis where ischaemic changes, possibly related to trauma and excess activity, cause avascular necrosis of the femoral head. It affects children between 6 and 12 who present with a limp and pain which again may be felt in the knee. There is pain and limitation of hip movement. X-rays reveal the typical changes of patchy bone density and collapse, with distortion of the femoral head. These cases are best managed by orthopaedic surgeons.

Stress fracture of the femur

This occurs as an overuse injury in runners less frequently than the stress fractures in the lower leg and metatarsals. It is usually associated with a recent increase in mileage. Twelve weeks off running are required to heal a femoral stress fracture.

Osteogenic sarcoma of the femur

The peak age incidence for this tumour is 18–25 and occasionally it presents as pain of sudden onset during sport. It is very important that when there is bony tenderness or bony swelling of the femur, an X-ray should be taken, as prompt diagnosis and treatment may be life saving.

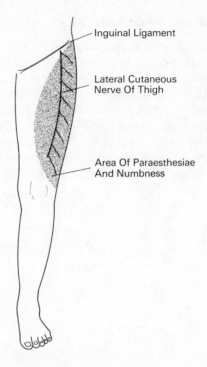

Inguinal Ligament

Lateral Cutaneous Nerve Of Thigh

Area Of Paraesthesiae And Numbness

Fig. 10.3. Meralgia paraesthetica.

NERVES

Meralgia paraesthetica

This syndrome is due to irritation or neuropraxia of the lateral cutaneous nerve of the thigh, causing tingling, numbness and pain down the antero-lateral aspect of the thigh (see Fig. 10.3). The symptoms are produced by a blow to or compression of the nerve at the lateral end of the inguinal ligament. It may be due to tight clothing or to pressure from protective padding. Once the cause has been removed, the symptoms resolve over the course of a few weeks.

Sciatica and referred lumbo-sacral pain

Irritation of the sciatic nerve may cause pain throughout the distribution of the nerve from the buttock and back of the thigh, down the lateral aspect of the calf, and into the foot, or only in parts of the distribution. There may be areas of numbness and motor weakness consistent with a sciatic lesion (see Fig. 10.4).

Referred pain from joints and ligaments in the lumbo-sacral region may be felt in the groin and thigh. Such pain is distributed in dermatomes and may be bilateral. Examination of the back will usually reveal spasm and limitation of movement.

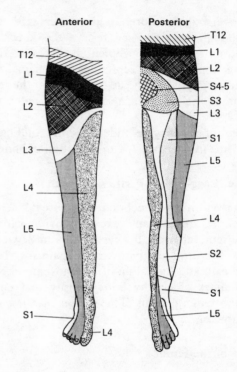

Fig. 10.4. Dermatomes of the hip and leg.

11
The Pelvis

PUBIC SYMPHYSITIS

This is rarely seen, except in professional footballers. Repetitive running and kicking may stress the pubic symphysis so that it weakens, allowing movement between the ends of the pubic rami. This causes severe pain on running or tilting the pelvis, the pain being referred bilaterally to the groin. There may be local tenderness over the symphysis. X-ray may show distraction and resorption of bone ends. Surgery is usually required to fuse the pubic bones at the symphysis. (This syndrome also occurs in the later stages of pregnancy, as hormonal changes cause softening of ligaments. In this case it recovers spontaneously after delivery.)

STRESS FRACTURES OF THE PUBIC RAMUS

These occasionally occur in runners. As with other stress fractures, they tend to be associated with a recent increase in mileage. Twelve weeks off running is required for sound healing.

ILIAC APOPHYSITIS

The apophysis on the iliac crest is the site of insertion for a number of strong trunk muscles. Excessive tugging on these origins during adolescence may cause symptoms of pain and tenderness, due to stress on the growth plate of the iliac crest, and in long-standing cases X-rays may reveal disruption of the bone of the apophysis.

The external oblique abdominal muscle arises from the anterior half of the iliac crest (see Fig. 11.1). This muscle is used in running especially in runners who swing their arms too much across their

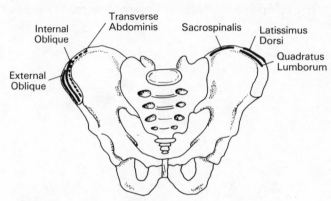

Fig. 11.1. Diagram to show muscle insertions into iliac crest.

bodies. Apophysitis of the anterior iliac crest can occur in adolescent runners — they are usually competing at middle distance and often have this fault in their technique. The symptoms settle with rest and the running technique should be corrected.

The latissimus dorsi, quadratus lumborum and sacrospinalis are attached to the posterior part of the iliac crest.

As with other apophyseal problems, the injury may recur until growth stops — usually between 17 and 20. The apophysis fuses anteriorly backwards.

SACRO-ILIAC PAIN

Pain and superficial tenderness felt in the sacro-iliac region are usually referred from the low lumbar spine, and a thorough examination of the back should be done.

The sacro-iliac joint has large congruous surfaces, bound together by massive ligaments, and it is difficult to imagine a sprain occurring, unless there is major trauma such as the pelvis being run over by a motor vehicle.

If the sacro-iliac joint is sprained or inflamed, this can be elicited by pelvic compression which will cause local pain in the joint. The most likely reason for this in someone who has not been in a road traffic accident is sacro-iliitis due to ankylosing spondylitis or Reiter's syndrome. An X-ray will reveal typical erosive or sclerotic changes which are usually bilateral. In early cases there may be no X-ray changes, but a technetium bone scan will reveal bilateral hot spots.

12

Abdomen and Lumbar Region

MUSCLE STRAINS

Quadratus lumborum

This muscle may be strained in activities involving back extension (e.g. rowing (including lifting boat in and out of the water) and weight-lifting). Pain is felt to one side of the lumbar region (see Figs. 12.1 and 12.2). Tenderness is palpable in the muscle belly somewhere between the iliac crest and the lower ribs. The muscle may be in spasm. It is a big muscle, and once the initial inflammation has settled, return of function is excellent.

Latissimus dorsi

This muscle has a wide origin from the posterior iliac crest, lumbar fascia, the spines of the lower six thoracic vertebrae, the three lowest ribs and the angle of the scapula (see Figs 12.1 and 12.2). It is inserted into the bicipital groove of the humerus, and it adducts, extends and medially rotates the humerus making it important in rowing and in climbing. Local tenderness can be elicited over the damaged fibres and resisted movement causes increased pain.

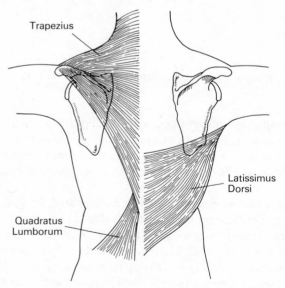

Fig. 12.1. Diagram showing some back muscles.

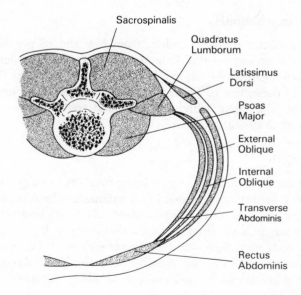

Fig. 12.2. Diagrammatic section through the trunk to show muscles.

Abdominal muscles

The rectus abdominis is occasionally sprained by activities involving flexion against resistance, e.g. rowing. Divarication of the recti may occur as a result of repetitive massive increases in intra-abdominal pressure, e.g. weight-lifting.

The internal and external oblique abdominal muscles are sometimes damaged by forced rotational movements in contact sports (see Fig. 12.2).

LUMBAR SPINE

Lumbar spine problems occur quite frequently in various sports, different types of injury predominating at different ages.

Hyperextension injuries

These are commonest in children from 6–9 and in people with hypermobile spines — this latter group often have evidence of generalised ligamentous laxity. Muscle spasm masks the hypermobility at presentation. There is diffuse tenderness, and impaired movement. Treatment with local heat and rest is followed by a programme to strengthen peripheral muscles.

Spondylolysis

This is a stress fracture of the pars interarticularis, usually affecting L5 or L4. It is peculiar to humans and is thought to be related to the upright position. It is often symptom-free, and it may be detected by chance when an X-ray is taken for another purpose. If bilateral, the vertebral body may slip forward on the vertebra below because it has become separated from the posterior complex of ligaments and apophyseal joints which stabilise the vertebrae — spondylolisthesis (see Fig. 12.3).

The condition is not present at birth, but has been found in infants

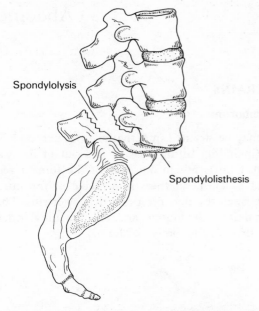

Fig. 12.3. Bilateral spondylolysis with spondylolisthesis at L5.

of 18 months, and its prevalance rises during childhood, reaching 5% in the adult population. In symptom-free gymnasts the incidence is 10%, and it is also high in ballet dancers. It may be the increased lumbar lordosis allowed by the defect confers an advantage for these activities.

It may cause symptoms, usually precipitated by great physical activity. It is not certain whether this is due to an acute fracture, or to movement in an already existing fracture. The onset may be sudden with a pain in the buttock so sharp it halts the victim, or there may be a prehistory of gradually increasing pain on exercise.

Symptoms may be seen in gymnasts as young as 5–7, and are due to the stresses imposed by hyperextension and lateral flexion, e.g. in back walkovers. In teenagers it is seen in association with rugby, football, squash or butterfly stroke. Typically, they are over-training (often with weights) and playing competitively several times a week. In the late teens and early twenties, it is seen in tennis players and cricket fast-bowlers. The initial hyperextension followed by forced flexion to serve or deliver the ball stresses the low lumbar region asymmetrically. The history is suggestive, and on examination, muscle spasm may be so severe that movements of the lumbar spine are virtually absent; however, if there is any movement, there is usually asymmetry of lateral flexion. With the patient prone, deep pressure over the vertebral spine of L4 or L5 will elicit the pain.

Oblique X-rays of the low lumbar region reveal the fracture and whether it is unilateral or bilateral. If bilateral, the lateral X-ray will show if there is any degree of spondylolisthesis.

Treatment is initially conservative. Rest and analgesics usually alleviate the pain and spasm, but sometimes immobilisation in a plaster jacket may be necessary for 4–6 weeks. When the pain has settled, swimming is allowed (except butterfly) but other sport should be avoided for 3 months. On return to sport, player, parents and coach should be advised to avoid over-training.

Sometimes the stress fracture heals. More often it does not, so that symptoms are likely to recur with over-activity. Where the defect is bilateral, there is a risk of spondylolisthesis occurring, especially during the growing years. It is said that once growth has stopped, further slip is unlikely to occur. All children with a bilateral spondylolysis with or without spondylolisthesis should be referred to an orthopaedic surgeon with a special interest in the spine. If slip is occurring, it may be necessary to stabilise the vertebrae.

Scheuermann's disease

This is an osteochondritis of the vertebral end-plate, affecting 10–16 year olds, and most frequently affecting the middle and lower thoracic spine and the upper lumbar spine. Damage to the vertebral end-plate results in abnormal growth with wedging of the vertebra causing a dorsal kyphosis and an exaggerated lumbar lordosis; less often lateral wedging may cause scoliosis. In addition there may be platyspondyly and the disc may distort or rupture the vertebral end-plate, causing the radiological appearance of Schmorl's nodes. The anterior part of the epiphyseal ring may become detached, and in severe cases anterior bridging between vertebral bodies may occur (see Fig. 12.4).

There is a familial form of the condition which is usually pain free, where the typical round-shouldered appearance of adolescent kyphosis develops silently in the mid to late teens.

In other teenagers, the onset may be painful and is associated with activities producing spinal compression, such as rowing, weight-lifting and playing forward at rugby, or the repetitive jarring and compression of long distance running. The pain may be quite severe, and may not be relieved by lying down. There may be paravertebral spasm, and there is tenderness on deep palpation over several vertebrae in the affected region. The X-ray may be normal initially, but later the changes described above develop. A technetium scan will show a characteristic hot patch. A normal white cell count and differential and erythrocyte sedimentation rate excludes the possibility of infection.

Recovery may take several months. When the pain has settled, swimming and light activity is allowed, but return to other sports should not be hurried. Structural damage already done cannot be reversed, but conservative measures should prevent further injury. Occasionally if kyphoscoliosis is increasing, a spinal brace may be necessary until growth is complete.

Once growth has stopped and the end-plate fused, no further damage to the vertebrae occurs, but the distortion of shape may be such that it predisposes the individual to mechanical backache in adult life. If this occurs, counselling should be given about avoiding activities such as heavy lifting. Attendance at a back class for instruction in posture and back exercises is helpful.

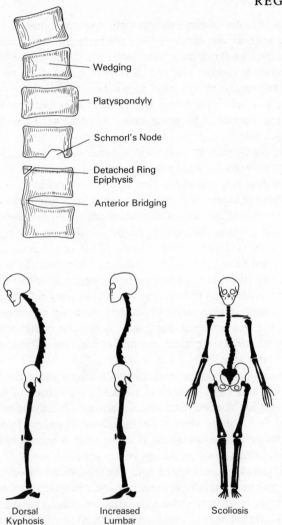

Wedging

Platyspondyly

Schmorl's Node

Detached Ring Epiphysis

Anterior Bridging

Dorsal Kyphosis

Increased Lumbar Lordosis

Scoliosis

Fig. 12.4. Late stages in Scheuermann's disease.

Vertebral fractures

Lumbar and dorsal fractures due to strong compressive forces such as trampolining and jumping from heights can cause vertebral body fractures. They can occur at any age, but seem to happen more readily in teenagers. Cervical fractures occur from falling on the head, e.g. in riding accidents, or falls in hyperflexion or hyperextension, e.g. rugby and gymnastics. There is a great danger of spinal cord injury. X-rays of the neck will reveal potentially unstable fractures. These require immediate immobilisation, and urgent referral to an orthopaedic surgeon for stabilisation.

Stress fractures of dorsal vertebral spines may occur due to excessive muscular contraction, e.g. C7 may be avulsed by weight-training or tennis, due to strong pulling from the insertions of the trapezius.

Traumatic fractures of transverse processes of the lumbar vertebrae (usually L1 or 2) may be caused by a blow in the loin. This is a very painful injury with marked muscle spasm and local tenderness. X-ray reveals the fracture. The kidney lies in this region and may also be damaged. The patient should be asked if there has been any haematuria, and a specimen of urine should be examined under the microscope for red cells.

Lumbar prolapsed intervertebral disc

In the adult spine, the weakest part of the vertebral body-disc complex is the annulus fibrosus (see Fig. 12.4). Compression forces to the spine such as bending or lifting may cause tears, weakening or rupture of the annulus fibrosus, with protrusion of the nucleus pulposus. Off-balance twisting movements may also tear the annulus fibrosus. The protrusion of disc contents may be sudden, causing sudden onset of pain and spasm, and an inability to straighten. It may also occur gradually over 24 hours, following a tear as the semi-liquid nucleus pulposus oozes out, causing gradual onset of pain and spasm.

The annulus fibrosus contains no pain endings, but the surrounding ligaments do, and it is pressure on these that gives rise to pain, and spasm of the paraspinal muscles. Stimulation of nerve endings in the ligaments may cause referred pain in the buttocks. If the protrusion impinges on the spinal nerve root, compression of nerve fibres causes pain and motor and/or sensory disturbance in the area supplied by the nerve. These symptoms may occur throughout the territory of the nerve supply, or only in part of it. Pain is usually present, but is not always so.

Numbness and paraesthesiae may predominate, or sometimes motor weakness may be the presenting symptom. Bilateral root symptoms and signs suggest a posterior protrusion, with the danger of further massive protrusion compressing the cord or cauda equina.

Coughing or sneezing typically exacerbate root pain — the cough impulse.

The discs which are subjected to maximal pressure and are most likely to be damaged are those at L4/5 and L5/S1 levels.

Clinically, the patient may have great difficulty in moving about, due to spasm of the paravertebral muscles. Sitting may be painful or impossible, and activities involving forward flexion such as putting on socks may be very difficult. Spasm causes the paravertebral muscles to stand out — they are tense on palpation. There is usually no palpable tenderness, although sometimes firm pressure over a vertebra may cause discomfort. Whilst severe muscle spasm persists, back movements are virtually absent. As the spasm subsides, limited movement returns and the patient can then be tested formally. It is best to stand behind the patient and watch the lumbar spine as the range of flexion, extension and lateral flexion are measured. A useful sign is to look for impairment of the curve made by the dorsal spines on lateral flexion — a segment of two or three vertebrae may be held straight on flexing to one side, whilst the curve develops smoothly on flexing to the other side. This appearance is due to local spasm of the short intervertebral slips of paravertebral muscles and indicates mechanical problems in the disc/vertebral complex. Straight leg raising pulls on the lower roots of the lumbar plexus, and is usually limited, particularly on the side to which the disc has prolapsed; however, with high lumbar disc lesions, straight leg raising may be unimpaired.

Forward flexion of the neck (the barber's chair sign) pulls on the dura and arachnoid maters and increases pain locally, where a disc protrusion is irritating them. Naffziger's test, in which the external jugular veins are compressed, so raising the pressure in the arachnoid venous plexus, causes pain at the level of an acute posterior or posterolateral disc protrusion.

The neurological examination of the leg indicates the presence and level of nerve root compression. An absent or depressed ankle jerk means a S1 lesion, whilst an absent knee jerk means a lesion of L4. Sensory testing of dermatomes and testing the power of muscle groups gives further information.

Straight and lateral X-rays of the lumbar area should be taken. In a young person with no previous history of back problems, the only abnormality may be straightening of the lumbar lordosis due to muscle spasm. In an older person, the presence of degenerative changes and disc space narrowing indicate previous stress. Congenital abnormalities predisposing to disc herniation such as asymmetrical segmentation at the lumbo-sacral junction or spina bifida occulta can be identified. It also shows any other bony abnormalities such as metastatic tumours, myeloma, tuberculous infection and old Scheuermann's disease. Computer Tomography, if available, gives a clear picture of the discs and any protrusions.

A patient with bilateral sciatica or difficulties with sphincter control probably has a posterior prolapse with the risk of imminent further prolapse, causing paralysis of the cauda equina and permanent incontinence. Such patients should be referred very promptly to a neurosurgeon for evaluation and decompression if necessary.

Apart from this rare problem, most patients require a period of bed rest to offload the lumbar spine and reduce the pressure on the intervertebral discs. This results in decreasing pain and muscle spasm. The majority improve rapidly in 3–4 days, but a larger prolapse may require up to 2 weeks rest. The patient should lie flat, with one pillow. If the bed sags, a board under the mattress may be beneficial, but the group of patients who have increased pain on extension will be less comfortable on a hard bed. Initially the patient may be allowed to get up to use the toilet, but should lie down the rest of the time, including meal-times. Once the spasm has decreased, the patient may be encouraged to get up and walk around the room at intervals, and to sit up for meals.

When reasonable mobility is restored, the patient may benefit from physiotherapy. Heat and gentle exercises are always beneficial — in some cases mobilisations and manipulations are helpful. A graded programme of exercises should be given to strengthen the spinal muscles, and attendance at back care classes to learn lifting and bending techniques helps prevent further incidents. Swimming regularly is an excellent way of mobilising and strengthening the back. It is likely to take 4–6 weeks at least to return to normal everyday activities, and as it takes 4 months for scar tissue to become maximally strong, really strenuous activity such as heavy lifting, rugby or squash should be avoided during this time.

A lumbar corset does not immobilise the back, but it provides some support, and is probably most useful because by restricting movement, it provides a constant reminder to the wearer to be careful.

People who are opposed to or bored with bedrest can be put in a plaster jacket and allowed some mobility. This should be left on for at least 6 weeks, provided it is tolerated.

Analgesics are required initially and a mild muscle relaxant such as meprobamate or diazepam (also sedative) is useful at night. NSAIDs reduce the soft tissue swelling and may make a marked difference to the symptoms, so they should be started early and continued for 2–3 weeks.

Congenital abnormalities

There are some variants of anatomical structure which normally cause no symptoms and are only discovered when seen on an X-ray of the spine. Under the excessive stresses generated by competitive sport, some of these conditions may give rise to mechanical back pain. As these appearances are considered to be insignificant, not all radiologists mention them in their reports, and this is one reason why one should look oneself at all X-rays.

VARIANTS OF SEGMENTATION

In embryonic development, segmentation starts at the head end and proceeds caudally, as the vertebrae develop from the mesoderm. The normal arrangement of 7 cervical, 12 thoracic, 5 lumbar and the sacral and coccygeal vertebrae fused to form sacrum and coccyx may be varied (see Fig. 12.6). There may be 6 free lumbar vertebrae due to T12 or S1 becoming lumbarised, or there may be only 4 due to the reverse process. Both of these conditions, i.e. 4 or 6 lumbar vertebrae, may be mechanically slightly disadvantageous.

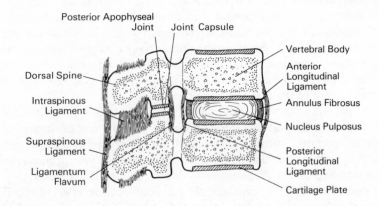

Fig. 12.5. Cross-section of spine.

The conditions that almost invariably cause problems are asymmetry at the lumbo-sacral junction where L5 or S1 is fused to the sacrum on one side and free on the other. Sometimes the top of the transverse process on one side may articulate with the ilium, while the other side lies free (see Fig. 12.6). In these situations, the asymmetrical anchoring imposes rocking forces on the lumbar-sacral region, and backache can be very troublesome. A prolapsed intervertebral disc above this is likely to occur due to the mechanical stresses.

SPINA BIFIDA OCCULTA

Spina bifida occulta of L5 or S1 is a common anomaly (see Fig. 12.6). It sometimes appears to be associated with referred pain in the back of the thigh in the S1/S2 distribution, e.g. in runners. It may also be associated with an increased tendency for a prolapsed intervertebral disc above or below the anomaly.

These conditions, as the other causes of mechanical back pain, respond to rest, NSAIDs, advice on back care and strengthening the back muscles by exercises or regular swimming.

Degenerative changes in the lumbar spine

With increasing age, the mucopolysaccharide of the nucleus pulposus polymerises and becomes less resilient. It resembles the consistency of toothpaste, rather than the jelly-like substance of earlier years. It also decreases in osmotic pull. The result is that the nucleus pulposus decreases in volume. Over the same period, the annulus fibrosus becomes laxer, partly because of decreased volume of the contained gel, and partly due to stretching of the collagen fibres. The end result is that the vertebrae sit closer on each other, so that there is an overall loss of height, the annulus fibrosus tends to bulge out around the vertebral margins, there is increased play in the anterior vertebral complex, and sprains and tears are more likely. The

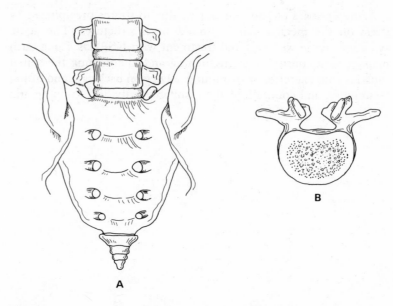

Fig. 12.6. Complications of the L5 disc. A. Asymmetry B. Spina bifida occulta.

tugging of the annulus fibrosus on the vertebral margin tends to cause the formation of osteophytes.

These changes in turn put more stress on the apophyseal joints in the posterior vertebral complex, and these, being synovial joints, develop osteoarthritic changes. Their ligaments become laxer, osteophytes form and sprains become more likely.

On examination, there may be altered configuration with diminished lumbar lordosis or a slight scoliosis. Movements may be restricted. Inflamed apophyseal joints are tender locally on deep palpation directly over the joint. X-ray is needed to assess the extent of degenerative changes.

Acute episodes of pain are usually due to strains precipitated by stress on the mechanically unsound worn structures. The acute symptoms settle with rest and treatment with NSAIDs. Long-term management consists of strengthening and maintaining the spinal muscles with exercises or swimming, advice on back care and lifting techniques, and counselling about suitable activities. Running and jogging are jarring activities and bad for the lower back, whereas walking, cycling and swimming are likely to be tolerated well. Squash, which involves a great deal of bending and twisting, is more likely to cause problems than badminton and tennis, which are played more upright.

QUEEN E... CANCELLED ...RARY,
CENTRAL BIRMINGHAM ... OF PHYSIOT...
HEALTH DIST...

BREAST PROBLEMS

Joggers' nipple

In women discomfort may arise from excessive movement of the breasts during running. This movement may cause friction between the nipple and overlying clothes causing local tenderness and swelling. It can be prevented by wearing a firm supportive bra.

Irritation of the nipple with inflammation causing enlargement of the breast pad occasionally occurs in men who wear braces, or some type of body harness which rubs in this region.

Women with large breasts may develop pain and soreness after running, due to shearing in the connective tissues. This can also be prevented by wearing a firm elasticated sports bra.

MUSCLES

Most of the muscles in the thoracic region are involved in shoulder movements, and transmission of power to or from the arm. The sterno-clavicular joint is the only skeletal link between the upper limb and the trunk. It has muscles which bind the scapula and upper limb to the trunk. These are particularly stressed in activities where the arms are lifting weight, or where the arms are fixed and the trunk raised, as in gymnastic exercises on rings and parallel bars, climbing ropes and rock climbing.

Pectoralis major

This muscle can be sprained by movements involving sustained or resisted shoulder flexion. There tends to be diffuse tenderness in the muscle where it overlies the upper ribs. Rarely the muscle fibres or tendon of the upper part ruptures completely, the muscle retracts, forming a lump over the upper ribs and there may be a palpable hollow lateral to this. Some function is retained as the other shoulder flexor muscles take the load, but there is insufficient strength for power activities (see Fig. 13.1).

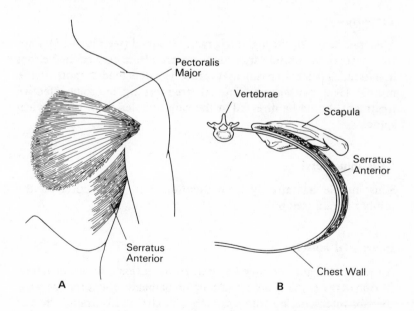

Fig. 13.1. A. Front of the chest. B. Horizontal section through the chest.

95

Serratus anterior

This muscle holds the scapula against the dorsal ribs, draws it laterally and stabilises the scapula when the upper limb is in use. Paralysis of the muscle, due to damage to its motor nerve, causes winging of the scapula. The muscle may be strained particularly by rowing.

Rhomboids

The rhomboids hold the medial borders of the scapulae in adduction, resisting rotation and elevation of the scapula.

Trapezius

This muscle is very strong and is rarely strained (see Fig. 12.1). Pain and spasm in the muscle are usually referred from cervical nerve root irritation, and local spasm may cause isolated tender spots in the muscle. Heat, massage and frictions are soothing, but to be effective treatment should be directed at the causative lesion in the cervical spine.

Latissimus dorsi

This muscle has already been mentioned in the section on the lumbar region (see p. 87).

Intercostal muscles

An intercostal muscle may be strained by excess rotation or lateral flexion of the trunk. There is usually no palpable tender spot because the ribs intervene, but there is pain on extreme inspiration, forced expiration and coughing. It has to be differentiated from a fractured rib. A sprained intercostal muscle recovers spontaneously in 7–10 days.

BONES

Fractured ribs

Compression of the thorax by a heavy weight, for instance at the bottom of a scrum, compresses the ribs and may cause one or more fractures, usually on the lateral curved aspect of the ribs. Sometimes a spontaneous rib fracture results from extremely forceful contractions of one of the scapular muscles inserted into a rib.

On examination there is local tenderness on palpation. After about 10 days, a protuberance due to callus may be palpable. Any activity causing movements of the ribs increases the pain, e.g. deep breathing, coughing and laughing. There may be crepitus audible through a stethoscope due to movement between the rough bone ends. The chest should always be examined to make sure there is no underlying collapse, or pneumothorax due to puncture of the lung. A recent fracture does not always show up on X-ray, but after 10 days is usually obvious due to presence of callus.

An isolated rib fracture is well splinted by the neighbouring ribs, and strapping is not necessary. The patient should be advised to take things quietly to avoid excessive rib excursion, and analgesics may be necessary initially. After 10 days, callus begins to unite the bone ends, so that pain decreases markedly, but coughing remains painful for 3 weeks, when the callus becomes really firm.

Stress fracture of ribs

Stress fracture of ribs may occur due to repetitive contraction of strong muscles inserted into the ribs, e.g. pectoralis major in the upper anterior ribs, serratus anterior and abdominal external oblique inserted into lateral lower ribs. Treatment is rest, as above.

Lesions of the thoracic spine

Due to the splinting effect of the ribs, the only significant movement occurring at the thoracic spine is rotation, which causes a shearing force on the intervertebral disc and gliding at the synovial apophyseal joints.

Apophyseal joint problems

Extreme rotation, or prolonged partial rotation stresses the capsule of the apophyseal joint, which may tear or stretch, and allow the joint surfaces to move out of apposition. This causes pain and muscle spasm, and the joint surfaces are unable to glide back into place. Pain is felt locally, and may also be referred around the equivalent dermatome. The pain is increased by rotation, particularly in one direction. On examination, there is tenderness over the affected apophyseal joint. Symptoms can be relieved promptly by mobilisation — local heat or ultrasound is applied to relax spasm and then the joint can be mobilised so that the normal configuration is restored. It will be slightly sore for some days, due to inflammation of the damaged capsule, and will be likely to recur if stressed before the capsule has healed. Probably the capsule always remains slightly lax because recurrence is not unusual.

Thoracic prolapsed disc lesions

These are less common than in the cervical or lumbar spine, probably because less movement is allowed at the vertebral disc complex. When a disc does prolapse, it tends to be in the lower thoracic region, where the relatively immobile thoracic spine meets the mobile lumbar spine, or at the apex of a scoliosis or kyphosis, for instance in an individual who has damage from past Scheuermann's disease. In these positions, there is increased mechanical stress for structural reasons, and superimposed stress from movement may overstrain the annulus fibrosus and allow prolapse of disc contents. Pain may be felt over the spine, or through all or part of the distribution of the dermatome. If the nerve root is compressed, there will be demonstrable hypoalgesia.

Treatment consists of rest, NSAIDs and analgesics. Good posture, keeping the dorsal spine straight when sitting, helps relieve the pain. Recovery is often slow. Once the pain has gone, the paraspinal muscles should be built up with exercises.

Scheuermann's disease

In the thoracic spine, this condition may occur silently, the first manifestation being a gradually developing adolescent kyphosis due to impaired growth in height of the anterior vertebral bodies. This type of onset is common in the familial form. These individuals are more likely to suffer from mechanical strains at the apex of the kyphos, or where the curve joins the normal lower vertebrae, in the lower thoracic region or at the junction with the cervical region (see also section on lumbar spine, p. 89).

However, in other teenagers, the condition may be very painful, and appears to be related to trauma, e.g. weight-training, rowing and long-distance running all impose excessive stress on the adolescent spine. In other cases, the precipitating cause appears to be postural, e.g. riding a racing bike with the handle bars set too low.

Although the lesion is in the vertebral bodies, there is often superficial tenderness over the dorsal spines and interspinous ligaments, and there is marked muscle spasm. The pain is exacerbated by sitting and standing, but in the acute stage is not always relieved by lying down.

X-rays may show nothing initially, but after some weeks the typical changes are seen with fragmentation of the epiphyseal ring, sometimes detachment of the anterior ring, wedging of the vertebra or vertebrae due to impaired anterior growth and platyspondyly. Technetium scan will reveal a hot patch over the involved vertebrae. The blood count is normal, but should be done to exclude other conditions, especially infection or tumour.

Bed rest may be necessary initially, with analgesics, and the pain may take several weeks to subside. It is important to see the child regularly to ensure no other condition is developing, and also to maintain morale. As the pain subsides, a programme of gentle mobilising and strengthening exercises should be begun. Recurrences of pain are frequent, so it is wise to keep the child off sport, with the exception of swimming, for up to 6 months. Very occasionally severe deformity develops, and a Milwaukee or equivalent spinal brace is required during the remaining years of growth to limit this.

Avulsion injuries of spinous processes

Extreme or repetitive stress on the insertions of the trapezius muscle into the dorsal spinal processes may cause apophysitis or even avulsion of the tip of the process. This may occur in teenagers while weight-lifting (particularly repetitions) or overplaying racquet sports. Rest from the precipitating cause is essential, and physiotherapy in the form of ice and ultrasound is helpful. Recovery may take up to 3 months.

14

The Shoulder and Upper Arm

Sports injuries of the upper limb are more likely to damage the dominant arm.

LOCAL FACTORS

Movements at the shoulder involve synchronous movements at the sterno-clavicular, acromio-clavicular and gleno-humeral joints co-ordinated with movements of the scapulae on the thoracic wall. Injury at any one of these joints affects this synchronisation and puts stress on the other joints.

The sterno-clavicular joint is a synovial joint with a fibro-cartilage meniscus. The capsule and ligaments hold it in apposition. The acromio-clavicular joint is also synovial with facetal surfaces lying obliquely in an upward and lateral direction. Gliding movements are limited by the acromio-clavicular ligament and the coraco-clavicular ligament.

The gleno-humeral joint allows a wide range of movement because the spherical humeral head articulates with the relatively small and flat glenoid cavity. The socket is deepened by the fibro-cartilaginous labrum, but there is very little mechanical stability in the joint. The capsule is weak, and it is the co-ordinated contractions of the muscles of the rotator cuff which maintain stability at this joint whilst allowing a wide range of movement. Paralysis or weakness of these muscles causes laxity of the gleno-humeral joint which may dislocate. Injury to the muscles causes pain and limitation of shoulder movement. Over the years they are subject to overuse, causing fibrosis and thickening of the tendons of the rotator cuff, and later degenerative changes. Superiorly the large multilocular sub-acromial bursa lies between the acromion and the humeral head — if it enlarges the tendon of supraspinatus becomes trapped. The tendon of the long head of biceps crosses the joint superiorly to be attached to the glenoid labrum.

MUSCLES

Rotator cuff injuries

The muscles of the rotator cuff are subscapularis anteriorly, supraspinatus and deltoid superiorly, infraspinatus and teres minor posteriorly (see Fig. 14.1). Supraspinatus and deltoid act together to

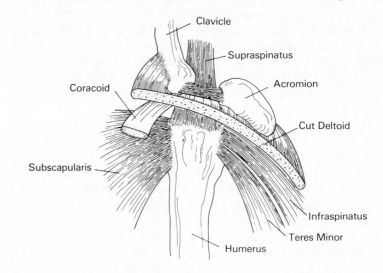

Fig. 14.1. Rotator cuff from lateral side.

produce abduction; their anterior fibres with the clavicular part of pectoralis major produce shoulder flexion, and their posterior fibres contribute to lateral rotation. The other short rotators — subscapularis, infraspinatus and teres minor — contract during these movements and hold the head of the humerus in the glenoid cavity.

The sports activities injuring the rotator cuff muscles are those involving gleno-humeral movement, e.g. serving and overhead shots in racquet sports, overarm bowling, crawl and butterfly swimming strokes, gymnastic and power weight-lifting.

Tears of the rotator cuff muscles cause pain and limitation of movement at the gleno-humeral joint. As the muscles closely invest the capsule, the inflammation may spread and a capsulitis develop so that there is palpable tenderness over the anterior joint line.

Treatment in the early stages is directed towards suppressing inflammation and preventing the development of a frozen shoulder. Ice, ultrasound, interferential or pulsed electromagnetic treatments are given with gentle pendular exercises. Oral NSAIDs are helpful. If there is evidence of capsulitis, an injection of hydrocortisone (50 mg) and local anaesthetic into the shoulder cavity through the anterior aspect is often helpful, and may be repeated twice at not less than fortnightly intervals. The patient should avoid all strenuous activities with the shoulder. As the pain settles, the pendular exercises can be replaced by strengthening exercises. Sport should not be recommended until the shoulder has a full pain-free range of movements.

A painful shoulder tends to be held in internal rotation and adduction. This disturbs the pattern of muscular tone around the shoulder girdle and often causes tension in the ipsilateral trapezius. In middle-aged and elderly subjects who have a degree of cervical spondylosis, this may precipitate an attack of neck pain with paraspinal spasm, and referred pain in the shoulder region augmenting the pain from the original injury. Recognition of the pattern and appropriate treatment of the cervical spine (see below) will break the vicious circle.

TENDONS

Supraspinatus tendinitis

That this is a common condition in the general population, and not just in athletes, reflects the amount of wear and tear imposed on the tendon (see Fig. 14.2). The nature of the changes in the tendon vary with age. It causes painful and limited abduction.

Children and teenagers may develop an acute inflammatory tendinitis due to overuse, e.g. intensive training for swimming or racquet sports.

In later life, chronic tendinitis due to overuse and perhaps aggravated by the impingement syndrome (see below) causes thickening and fibrosis of the tendon. The scar tissue has a tendency to

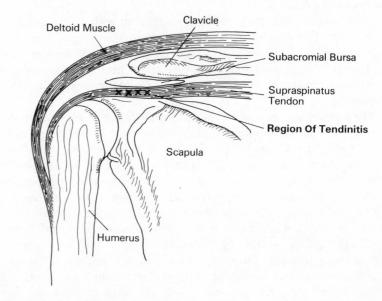

Fig. 14.2. Supraspinatus tendinitis.

calcify, and discrete masses of calcium salts are seen on X-ray. It is often seen in asymptomatic shoulders. Sometimes an acute attack of shoulder pain seems to coincide with extrusion of a mass of calcified material from the tendon.

In children, the acute tendinitis responds to rest and physiotherapy. Although infiltration of hydrocortisone around the tendon will relieve the symptoms, it may in the long term predispose to early degenerative changes. For this reason, it is probably wiser to avoid treating children and teenagers with steroid injections.

In older people, the symptoms often respond to NSAIDs and physiotherapy, but since degenerative changes are almost certainly already present, local steroid injection may sometimes be justifiably used to relieve symptoms. However, care should be taken not to inject it into the tendon, and no more than three injections of 50 mg hydrocortisone should be given within 6 months. The injection may be very painful — if mixed with local anaesthetic this relieves the initial discomfort, but when the effect wears off it may be very painful for 24–48 hours.

Tendon of long head of biceps

This may become inflamed where it lies in its synovial sheath in the bicipital groove on the head of the humerus going into the shoulder joint. Repetitive movements involving shoulder adduction and flexion combined with elbow flexion are particularly likely to cause bicipital tendinitis. It usually settles rapidly with rest, NSAIDs and physiotherapy. Occasionally an injection of hydrocortisone and local anaesthetic into the synovial sheath is required.

Repeated attacks of tendinitis weaken the tendon, which may rupture. Once this has happened, the pain goes, but there is an egg-shaped swelling over the upper arm due to retraction of the long head of biceps. Repairing may be possible if undertaken immediately. If not repaired function is still usually good.

BURSAE

Subacromial bursitis

In response to friction from repeated excursions of the supraspinatus tendon, the subacromial bursa may become enlarged and inflamed. This causes pain at the tip of the shoulder and a painful arc on abduction of the arm. The swollen, tender bursa may be palpated below the tip of the acromium.

It may resolve with a local injection of 50 mg hydrocortisone, and local anaesthetic into the bursa. The bursa is multilocular and the injection may need to be repeated up to three times. In athletes, persistent overuse may lead to chronic thickening of the bursa. This may require surgical excision of the bursa with or without acromioplasty.

Impingement syndrome

This syndrome is particularly a problem for middle-aged racquet sport players. Many regular players tend to develop a 'droop' of the shoulder of the racket arm as a postural habit. It is due to the laxity of the scapular elevating muscles allowing the scapula to rotate. This causes the tip of the acromion to impinge on the head of the humerus, trapping the supraspinatus tendon and acromial bursa, especially during overhead shots. The friction causes chronic inflammation of the bursa and fibrosis and thickening of the supraspinatus tendon. The symptoms are recurrent pain and stiffness, exacerbated by abduction. A co-existent weakness of the rotator cuff muscles due to repeated small tears will allow the humeral head to rise in the glenoid and increase the problem.

In the early stages, prevention and correction of the tennis droop by teaching shoulder-elevating exercises may be curative. Once changes of chronic inflammation have developed with thickening of the bursa and tendon, acromioplasty becomes necessary.

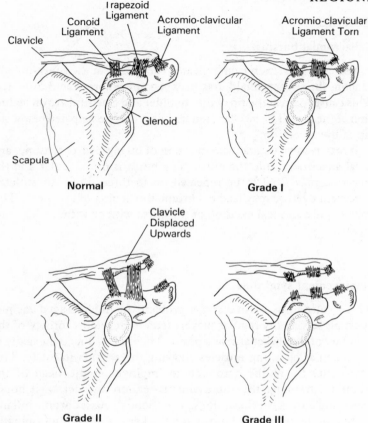

Fig. 14.3. Acromio-clavicular sprain and subluxations.

LIGAMENTS AND JOINTS

Injuries to the sterno-clavicular joint

Falling onto the arm, or lifting heavy weights above the head may sprain or even dislocate the sterno-clavicular joint, tearing the ligaments and capsule. There is pain and swelling over the joint, which is tender on palpation, and hurts when the arm is moved against resistance or the shoulder is elevated. It usually reduces spontaneously and the ligaments heal with local physiotherapy. Occasionally the joint remains unstable, giving pain whenever the arm and shoulder is moved, or if compressed by sleeping on that side. In this case surgical plication is necessary.

Acromio-clavicular sprain

This is quite a common injury, incurred by falling onto the point of the shoulder (see Fig. 14.3). This tears the acromio-clavicular and coraco-clavicular ligaments, which stabilise the joint, allowing springing of the lateral end of the clavicle. There is a painful, tender swelling over the acromio-clavicular joint, and pain on scapulo-thoracic movement. It is a common rugby injury, and also occurs in cyclists or horse-riders who fall off onto the shoulder. X-ray reveals the degree of distraction or dislocation.

The majority of cases become pain-free after physiotherapy for about 2 weeks. Ice and ultrasound help resolve the acute inflammation, and exercises to strengthen the muscles of the shoulder girdle offload the acromio-clavicular joint. Usually recovery of function is excellent, but the lateral end of the clavicle remains prominent. In the case of rugby players, symmetry is usually restored before long by a similar injury on the other shoulder! Very occasionally, if total ligamentous rupture occurs, the joint may remain unstable and painful. Surgical plication is then necessary.

Recurrent dislocation of the gleno-humeral joint

This may occasionally occur due to congenital laxity of the shoulder joint, e.g. in inherited disorders of connective tissue such as the Ehlers–Danlos syndrome. However, in sports players it usually follows initial severe trauma which dislocates the shoulder and tears the glenoid labrum. If this fails to heal, it leaves a weakness which allows recurrent dislocation of the humeral head with quite minor trauma.

The initial injury is most frequently anterior dislocation, the humerus having been forced into abduction and external rotation during a fall or tackle at contact sports. For successful reduction, muscle relaxation is required. Subsequent dislocations may be caused more and more easily by putting the arm into abduction and elevation — to start with this may happen again in a tackle, but with each episode the torn labrum and capsule become laxer, and the rotator cuff weakens, so that eventually it may pop out during totally unresisted movements, such as lifting the arm for the crawl stroke, or stretching the arm out to put a coat on. At the same time, reduction becomes much easier and will either occur spontaneously or be effected by the patient.

Following reduction or dislocation, the shoulder is painful and stiff, and there is tenderness along the joint line. Sometimes the circumflex nerve is damaged, causing paralysis of the deltoid and a patch of skin numbness on the top of the shoulder. Following the first dislocation, the shoulder should be immobilised by putting the arm in a sling for 3–4 weeks, and then mobilised slowly, with exercises to strengthen the shoulder muscles. Subsequent dislocations cause less tissue damage, and can be mobilised sooner.

Wearing a restraining harness to prevent abduction during play may prevent further dislocations, but many athletes find the limitation of movement interferes too much with play. If recurrent dislocation is seriously interfering with activity, surgery is required.

X-rays of the humeral head may show a posterior wedge defect caused by impingement on the glenoid rim during anterior dislocation. Arthrography is needed to demonstrate the position of the tear, or alternatively, arthroscopy may be used to locate the tear. Surgical strategy can then be planned to correct the defect.

Posterior dislocations occur less frequently. If recurrent, they also require surgery.

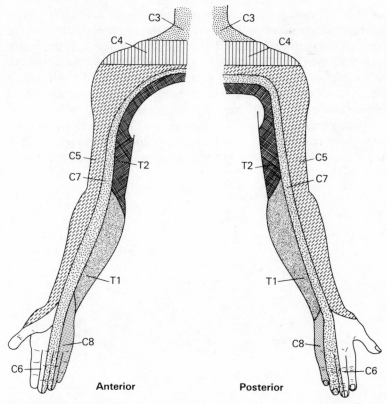

Fig. 14.4. Dermatomes of the arm.

NERVES

Brachial plexus traction injuries

Forced lateral flexion of the neck when the head is forced away from the shoulder pulls on the brachial plexus, causing damage. If the injury occurs at speed, as in a motor-cycle accident, severe lesions result, with avulsion of the nerve root from the cord, or neurotmesis (rupture) of the nerve root just distal to the intervertebral foramen. Prognosis here is poor, and a flail arm is the end result. If the injury happens due to a fall, for example at trampolining, or off a horse, the deceleration is much less. The pull on the cords of the brachial plexus is not enough to rupture them, although neurons and blood vessels inside the cord may be torn, causing local oedema and temporary loss of function — neuropraxia. The injuries affect the upper cord most frequently, causing neurological signs in the C5, 6 and 7 nerve roots, with loss of sensation, weak muscles and absent reflexes (see Fig. 14.4).

Symptoms due to local oedema in the nerve root will improve over the next few days, but those due to rupture of neurons will recover more slowly, if at all. The new nerve fibre grows along the sheaths at a rate of 1 mm a day. Electromyography is worth doing, if there has been no spontaneous improvement over the first 7–10 days, as it gives an indication of the prognosis. Even if some neurons do not regenerate, the return of muscle function is usually good, as motor units supplied by intact neurons hypertrophy. This is enhanced by exercises.

15
The Arm and Hand

SKIN

Blisters

Blisters are a recurrent problem for individuals using hand-held equipment such as racquets, bats and oars. They form on the pressure points of the palmar aspect over the heads of the metacarpals and the phalanges. Prevention and treatment is as described in Chapter 4. With time, the blisters heal and tend to be replaced by callus.

Calluses

These are largely protective thickening of the skin over friction points. If they become too thick, they may start to detach and tear the skin beneath, leaving a route for infection. In this case the calluses should be soaked and then rubbed with a pumice stone to keep them supple and of a reasonable thickness.

MUSCLES

(Lateral epicondylitis tennis elbow)

This common injury, despite its name, is by no means confined to the sporting population, but is even more common in people using their arms at work and for chores about the house. It is due to partial avulsion of the common extensor origin off the lateral humeral epicondyle. All the extensor muscles controlling wrist and fingers are inserted into quite a small area on the lateral epicondyle. A sudden resisted movement, or recurrent forced extension of the wrist, especially whilst gripping something in the hand, stresses this region

and tears muscle fibres off their insertion into the periosteum. If these stresses are repeated before healing is complete, the vascular granulation tissue will tear, causing local bleeding and more inflammation. Repetition of this process leads to the build-up of a knot of chronic inflammation. It can also be aggravated by bumping the lateral condyle on a doorway or some other hard object.

It is indeed a common injury in tennis and other racquet sports. The pain may occur only as a twinge, whilst gripping something and extending the wrist, or it may be continuous and quite severe. Sometimes it radiates up and down the arm. On examination, there is tenderness which may be localised to the common extensor origin on the lateral humeral epicondyle (Fig. 15.1), or it may become more diffuse, and extend into the upper muscle bellies of the extensor muscles. Picking up a chair with one hand typically exacerbates the pain. If it is long-standing, a lump of tender, chronic scar tissue may be palpable over the extensor origin.

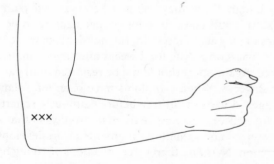

Fig. 15.1. Tenderness over the lateral epicondyle of the humerus.

There is no rapid cure for tennis elbow. If the patient is seen near the beginning of the first attack, treatment should be rest, preferably in a sling for 2 weeks with NSAIDs, followed by a further 2 weeks rest not in a sling, and then a cautious return to sport only after pain has been absent for at least 2 weeks. This regime gives a good chance of healing by primary intention. The sling is important, because it reminds the patient (and friends and relatives) to be careful and avoid everyday activities likely to aggravate the symptoms, e.g. picking up a file, or lifting a tin can off the shelf.

If symptoms have been present for some time, recovery is slower. Rest and NSAIDs are used together with physiotherapy in the form of ultrasound and friction to palpable knots of chronic fibrous tissue. In this case it is wise to insist on 4 weeks pain-free before returning to sport. A commercial tennis elbow splint, or a piece of half-inch wide (1 cm) zinc oxide tape bound firmly round the forearm an inch below the olecranon will take some of the load off the extensor origin.

Alternatively, a course of up to three injections of 50 mg hydrocortisone and local anaesthetic can be given at 2–4 weekly intervals. It is important to site the injection right on the insertion. To do this, palpate the point of maximal tenderness, push the needle in until it reaches bone, withdraw very slightly and infiltrate the area. The hydrocortisone will suppress the chronic scar tissue and relieve the pain (though there may initially be increased pain after the injection), but it still takes time for proper healing to occur. If the patient tries to play again too soon, further damage will occur. It is a good idea to insist on a sling for 2 weeks after injection, to give healing a chance. Again, sport should not be restarted until pain has been absent for 2 weeks. When symptoms have been long-standing, it is wise to suggest 4 weeks pain-free before cautiously restarting sport.

The hydrocortisone may cause dermal atrophy, so that an area of altered, depressed and sometimes pigmented skin develops over the area of injection. No more than three injections of 50 mg hydrocortisone (or equivalent) should be given within 6 months.

If the above measures in combination with extensive rest are not effective, the patient may be referred for surgery. There are various operations, but most depend on excising chronic scar tissue and attempting to get healing of muscle onto periosteum by first intention.

Preventative measures include the use of splints or taping, and altering the diameter of grip, the weight and the springiness of the racquet.

Medial epicondylitis (Golfers' elbow)

This is a similar condition to the above, but less common. It affects the common flexor origin on the medial epicondyle of the humerus. Management is as for lateral epicondylitis.

Aponeuroses

The aponeurotic insertion of the biceps may become sore and tender, usually as a result of fixed prolonged flexion of the elbow. It usually settles spontaneously with rest.

TENDONS

The extensor and flexor tendons in the forearm, wrist and dorsum of the hand are contained in synovial sheaths. Overuse may precipitate an episode of tenosynovitis.

Tenosynovitis of extensor carpi radialis

This is a common rowing injury, causing a tender sausage-shaped swelling on the radial side of the dorsum of the lower forearm. When acute, both patient and examiner can feel the creaking or crepitus on extension–flexion of the wrist. It usually occurs where the muscle belly of abductor pollicis longus crosses the tendon of extensor carpi radialis (see Fig. 15.2). This muscle contracts when the oar is gripped and compresses the underlying extensor tendon, increasing the

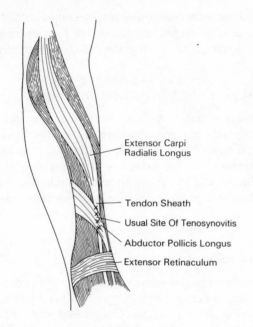

Extensor Carpi
Radialis Longus

Tendon Sheath

Usual Site Of Tenosynovitis

Abductor Pollicis Longus

Extensor Retinaculum

Fig. 15.2. Extensor tenosynovitis of the wrist.

friction as it glides up and down, due to the action of the wrist with each stroke. Beginners tend to grasp the oar unnecessarily tightly, thus precipitating an attack. More experienced rowers cup the oar without gripping hard, unless they are rowing in rough water. This, or else a succession of very long outings are what tend to trigger an attack in experienced rowers.

Usually, an acute attack subsides with rest, but ice and ultrasound, and oral NSAIDs are helpful. A simple wrist extensor splint will keep the tendon still — some people even manage to row wearing one of these. If recovery is slow, or a major contest is looming, the symptoms of pain and swelling are removed by injecting hydrocortisone into the tendon sheath and allowing it to run up and down the tendon — however, symptoms may recur during or after the race.

Occasionally, the synovitis becomes chronic, and in this case surgery to lay open the tendon sheath relieves symptoms rapidly, allowing a return to rowing within a few days. It does however leave a tell-tale scar.

De Quervain's tenosynovitis

This eponym refers to tenosynovitis of the extensor pollicis brevis tendon, or abductor pollicis longus (see Fig. 15.3), which may be

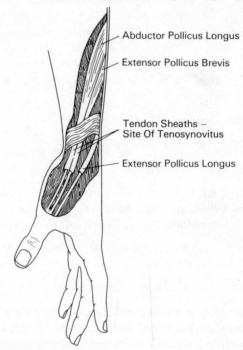

Abductor Pollicus Longus

Extensor Pollicus Brevis

Tendon Sheaths –
Site Of Tenosynovitus

Extensor Pollicus Longus

Fig. 15.3. De Quervain's tenosynovitis.

caused by gripping some object. There is tenderness around the base of the thumb in the snuff-box area, and pain is elicited on forced extension or abduction of the thumb. The condition responds to injection of hydrocortisone and rest.

Trigger finger or thumb

This is due to a thickening of one of the flexor tendons. The thickening is usually due to trauma. Typically, it catches at the distal end of the tendon sheath in the palm, so that the finger may get stuck in flexion and then suddenly go into extension as the knot is forced past the narrow end of the sheath. A similar situation exists on the palmar aspects of the fingers, where again the thickened tendon may catch at the opening of the synovial sheath. The jerky movement is characteristic, and the thickened knot in the tendon can be palpated. It is usually tender. Injection of a small quantity of hydrocortisone around the knot causes it to resolve.

LIGAMENTS

Torn medial ligament of elbow

This may be totally ruptured when the elbow is dislocated. After reduction, mobilisation should be very slow, as myositis ossificans is particularly likely to form in this area. Rapid mobilisation is thought to precipitate it.

Chronic medial ligament sprain of the elbow

Overarm throwing or bowling of a ball, or throwing a javelin with a partially flexed elbow is bad technique, as it stresses the medial ligament, causing pain and tenderness, and sometimes even calcification in the ligament.

The pain and tenderness are eased by physiotherapy but will recur unless technique is corrected and the elbow fully extended during throwing. Advice from the coach is needed to correct this.

Sprained wrist

Falling onto the wrists may tear the radial or ulnar collateral ligaments. X-rays will exclude a fracture. If the wrist is unstable, due to a total tear, it should be referred for orthopaedic management. If the wrist is stable, it can be treated with a simple wrist splint and gradual mobilisation. Such an injury may also bruise the articular disc on the ulnar side of the wrist joint, and this may remain tender for 2–3 months.

Interphalangeal joints

Injuries to the fingers from getting trapped in clothing or stamped on in a rugby scrum, or being struck end-on by a ball, may dislocate interphalangeal joints. These dislocations usually reduce spontaneously, but the damage to the ligaments causes bruising, swelling and stiffness. The joint may become quite swollen. X-rays will show if there is an associated fracture or avulsion.

Pain and swelling can be reduced by soaking in icy water, and the finger can be supported and mobilised by strapping it with zinc oxide tape to the adjacent finger, above and below the injured joint. Gentle movements should be encouraged to avoid permanent stiffness due to fibrosis. The joint often remains slightly thickened, and the patient should be warned of this.

Mallet finger

Forced flexion of the terminal digit may avulse the slip of extensor tendon inserted into the base of the terminal phalanx, so that the

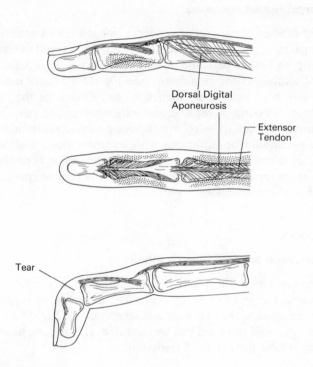

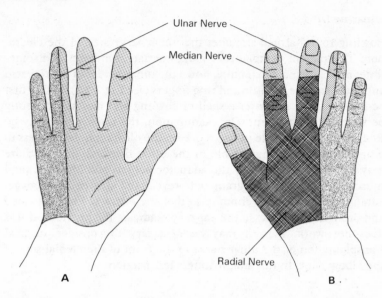

Fig. 15.5. Cutaneous territory of the nerves to the hand. A. Palmar aspect. B. Dorsal aspect.

Fig. 15.4. Mallet finger.

patient is unable to extend it (see Fig. 15.4). Attempts to sew the tendon back in place have not been successful, as it is too tenuous for sutures to grip. The only hope of cure is to put the finger as soon as possible into a hyperextension splint, and keep it hyperextended without fail for 6 weeks. Sometimes this allows the tendon to heal back in place. In no circumstances should patient or doctor be tempted to flex it to see how it is getting on during the intervening 6 weeks, as this will irretrievably disrupt any attempt at union.

NERVES

Radial palsy

A blow to the lateral side of the upper arm may damage the radial nerve, causing numbness and tingling in the dorsum of the hand and a wrist drop (see Fig. 15.5). The symptoms may be short-lived, but if neuropraxia has occurred, recovery will take several weeks. An electromyogram is useful to indicate the state and rate of recovery. An extensor wrist splint may be useful, as it will stabilise the wrist and facilitate finger function whilst the wrist extensors are out of action.

Ulnar neuritis

Bowling round-armed stretches the ulnar nerve around the olecranon. The patient complains of paraesthesiae, numbness and sometimes an aching pain extending down the ulnar border of the forearm and into the little, or little and ring fingers (see Fig. 15.5). It may first be noted during and after a spell of bowling and may subsequently become more persistent. On examination, the ulnar nerve may be thickened and palpable in its groove on the olecranon. Numbness to pinprick may be demonstrable in the ulnar distribution, and there may be motor weakness of the adductor pollicis and intrinsic hand muscles. An electromyogram will reveal the degree of damage. Attention to bowling technique so that the elbow is fully extended and brought over close to the ear may eradicate the problem. If this does not work, then it may be necessary to consider surgical transplantation of the ulnar nerve to the front of the medial side of the elbow joint. In this site, it suffers less friction.

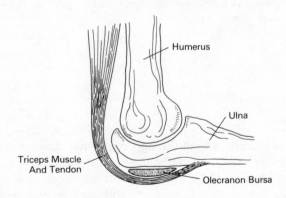

Fig. 15.6. Olecranon bursa at the elbow.

Carpal tunnel syndrome

The median nerve may be rendered ischaemic as it goes through the carpal tunnel if the wrist becomes swollen as a result of trauma. Early symptoms are of pain and paraesthesiae in the thumb, index, middle and sometimes the ring finger (see Fig. 15.5). Later numbness and weakness of extension, abduction and flexion of the thumb may occur. Wearing a ready-made extension splint may reduce the tension sufficiently to relieve the symptoms. Failing this, the carpal tunnel should be infiltrated with hydrocortisone and local anaesthetic to reduce oedema. Surgical decompression is rarely necessary in acute traumatic cases as the symptoms resolve spontaneously as the swelling decreases.

BURSA

Olecranon bursitis (miner's elbow)

The olecranon bursa may become inflamed as a result of repeated trauma, e.g. jerky extension as in dart throwing, or repeated falling on the point of the elbow in contact sports (see Fig. 15.6). The bursa enlarges, and the fluid can be aspirated. If it recurs, hydrocortisone may inhibit further fluid formation.

BONES AND CARTILAGE

Ulceration of olecranon fossa

Repeated hyperextension of the elbow, as in bowling or pitching, may cause damage to the cartilage in the olecranon fossa of the humerus, where the olecranon impinges in full extension (see Fig. 15.7). This causes pain on full extension of the elbow, and with the elbow flexed, a tender area may be felt in the olecranon fossa.

The inflammation may settle with rest, physiotherapy and NSAIDs. If symptoms persist, the patient should be referred for

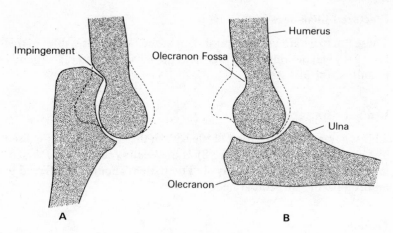

Fig. 15.7. The elbow. A. Extension. B. Flexion.

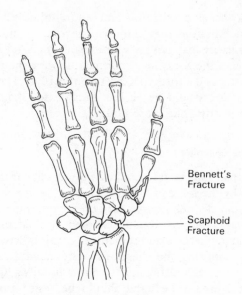

Fig. 15.8. Fractures of the hand.

surgery as there is probably a mass of scar tissue or even an ulcerated area of cartilage. Surgical removal of these, followed by a slow return to activity gives an excellent result.

Osteochondritis of the capitulum

This condition develops in 8–16 year olds and appears to be related to trauma. It is common in young gymnasts where repeated handstands or vaulting force the radial head against the capitulum. There is local tenderness and the elbow may develop fixed flexion. In the early stages, X-rays are normal, but later patchy density in the capitulum may develop, due to areas of bone necrosis, and the shape may become distorted. Treatment consists of rest and gentle exercises. Ultrasound may relieve the tenderness. The condition settles slowly and often takes up to 6 months to get better. If radiological changes have developed, they may gradually regress.

In the late teens and twenties, osteochondritis dissecans of the capitulum may cause symptoms due to detached fragments of bone

with overlying cartilage causing locking of the joint. X-ray may reveal the loose bodies, but sometimes the bony fragment may have died whilst the cartilage has gone on growing. Such loose bodies will not be visible on plain X-ray but will show up with arthrography. Surgical removal is necessary. The loose bodies are usually multiple, and more may form, requiring further surgery. The condition is often bilateral, and is thought to be related to trauma, as it is common in physically active youngsters.

Fractured scaphoid

Any person who has fallen onto an extended hand and is tender in the anatomical snuffbox should be suspected of having a scaphoid fracture (see Fig. 15.8). The danger of the fracture is that the distal fragment may become ischaemic and fail to unite. It is possible that prompt immobilisation may improve the rate of union. Unfortunately, the fracture may not always be visible on X-ray immediately; therefore even if the X-ray looks normal, the wrist should be put in a scaphoid plaster and a further X-ray taken in 10 days later, by which time the fracture would be visible. Such cases should always be referred to a fracture clinic promptly.

Fractured metacarpals

The metacarpals may be fractured by a direct blow from a cricket or hockey ball, by the force of a karate chop or by boxing without the hands being taped. Such injuries turn up not infrequently at a Sports Injury Clinic. There is usually marked haematoma formation, localised bony tenderness and sometimes crepitus between the bone ends. X-ray confirms the diagnosis. The metacarpals are well-splinted by the neighbouring bones, so that usually a light support is all that is required. The hand should be rested from strenuous activity for 4 weeks.

Fractured phalanges

These fractures are usually spiral, so that the fracture is stable. In this case, they can be splinted by taping to the adjacent finger, and gently mobilised for 3–4 weeks.

Bennett's fracture

This is a fracture/dislocation of the base of the thumb usually caused by forced abduction (see Fig. 15.8). If there is any suspicion of this injury the hand should be X-rayed. The patient should be referred to an orthopaedic surgeon at once.

Ganglia

These thin-walled cysts develop on the dorsum of the hand or wrist, often in association with repetitive trauma. They are outpouchings of the synovium in the wrist joint or tendon sheaths, and their contents are jelly-like, as they contain mucopolysaccharides. If they interfere with function, they should be removed by careful surgical dissection. The contents are too viscous for aspiration. The old-fashioned cure was to hit them with the family Bible. This disperses the contents temporarily, but they reform.

SKIN

Cuts

The skin of the face and head has a rich blood supply, and bleeds profusely from cuts. However, this plentiful blood supply also means that wounds heal quickly. Abrasions must be cleaned and any debris removed. Lacerations can usually be closed with butterfly sutures, which have the advantage of no additional scars from stitch holes. More extensive wounds may need careful suturing, whenever possible by a plastic surgeon.

Bruises

Haematomas tend to be large, due to the copious blood supply. On the face and neck the haemorrhage tracks through the skin and pools in lax areas, e.g. around the orbit. On the scalp the subcutaneous layers are tight, and localise the haematoma, which tends to stand out as an egg. Local application of ice, either as a pack or by rubbing gently with an ice cube, speeds reabsorption of the haematoma.

CAULIFLOWER EAR

Friction or a blow to the ear occurs particularly in boxing, wrestling and rugby. It applies a shearing force to skin which is torn off the cartilage. Haemorrhage and exudate from the torn vessels accumulate in the helix, rendering the ear swollen and shapeless. It separates the fibrocartilage from the nutrient vessels in the skin, and if this persists for some days, the cartilage may become necrotic, and collapse. As a result, the pinna retracts and loses its shape, causing the typical cauliflower ear. To avoid this happening, the haematoma and exudate should be aspirated with a syringe, and then the ear should be packed and bandaged firmly to the head, to prevent reaccumulation of fluid. This should be maintained for 7–10 days. To avoid recurrence, the ear should be protected during sport by wearing a helmet or an ear-guard.

THE EYE

Eye injuries may cause abrasion or contusion of the globe with potentially serious consequences. They should always be referred immediately to an emergency eye clinic.

MUSCLES

Muscle injuries are rare in this site. Pain and spasm in the neck muscles are usually due to a problem with the cervical spine. Successful treatment depends on correct diagnosis of the underlying cause.

BONES

Broken nose

Immediate treatment of a broken nose is possible if the patient reaches an ENT surgeon before swelling has occurred. The extent of deformity and interference with function can then be assessed and necessary action taken. If the patient presents after swelling has

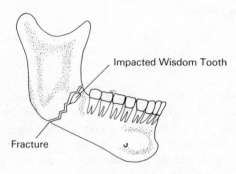

Fig. 16.1. Fracture of the mandible.

occurred, an X-ray can be taken to confirm the fracture, and an appointment made with an ENT surgeon in 5–7 days time. By this stage, the swelling will have subsided enough for the surgeon to decide if surgical correction is required on cosmetic or functional grounds. Delay in referral after the bone is beginning to set makes treatment difficult or impossible.

Fractured mandible

Impacted wisdom teeth weaken the mandible so that a relatively minor force, typically from a boxing or rugby injury, may fracture the mandible at this point (see Fig. 16.1). The victim may not realise what has happened, and present at the Soft Tissue Injury Clinic. On examination, there is localised tenderness, often marked swelling and trismus. X-ray confirms the diagnosis. This injury is in effect a compound fracture, so the patient should be put on penicillin and referred promptly to a dental surgeon.

As a prophylactic measure, it is wise for anyone with impacted wisdom teeth who boxes or plays contact sports to have them removed.

INJURIES TO THE CERVICAL SPINE

Fractures and dislocations

Fractures of the cervical spine occur particularly in falls with the head in flexion or in extension. Rupture of the paravertebral ligaments, or bilateral fracture of the vertebral arch results in instability and a risk of cord damage and tetraplegia (see Fig. 16.2). Sports particularly likely to cause such injury are gymnastics, trampolining, horse-riding, rugby and diving (see Fig. 16.3). In the majority of cases, the seriousness of the injury is recognised at once, and the patient has the neck immobilised and is taken straight to hospital. Occasionally someone with a potentially unstable fracture/dislocation walks away from the incident, and may later present with a stiff neck or neurological symptoms in the arm. This possibility should always be borne in mind when examining traumatic neck injuries. An X-ray should always be done, partly to screen for unstable

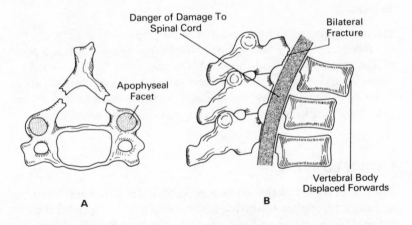

Fig. 16.2. Fractures of the cervical spine. A. Bilateral fracture of vertebral arch. B. Forward slip of vertebra with risk of damage to spinal cord.

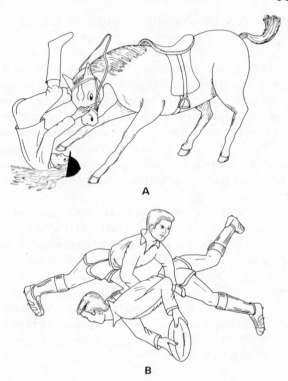

Fig. 16.3. Falls damaging neck. A. With neck in flexion. B. With neck in extension.

fracture/dislocation, but also to identify any other bony problems which might be contra-indications to mobilisation or manipulation, e.g. primary or metastatic tumours and osteophytes, especially those impinging on the intervertebral foramina. Mobilisation and manipulation should only be done by physiotherapists trained in these techniques. Amateur attempts at neck manipulation should be avoided.

Apophyseal joint problems

Forced rotation or lateral flexion stress the apophyseal joints (Fig. 16.4) so that the facets may be pulled apart, or slid across each other. This tends to tear or stretch the capsule, and when the force is removed, the surfaces may remain misaligned. This distorts the capsule and surrounding ligaments, generating acute pain and spasm. The neck is stiff and may be pulled into torticollis. Neck movements may all be impaired, but there is usually asymmetry to the blocking of rotation and lateral flexion. Palpation from the posterior aspect over the apophyseal joints reveals local tenderness at the affected one. There may be some referred pain and spasm in the trapezius muscle, but there are no signs or symptoms of nerve root irritation.

The displacement is usually too slight to show on X-ray, but films

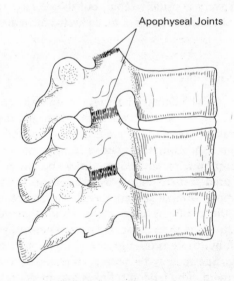

Apophyseal Joints

Fig. 16.4. Lateral view of cervical spine.

should be taken, to exclude any conditions likely to be aggravated by manipulation.

Treatment is by manipulation to restore the alignment of the apophyseal joint to normal. Relief is usually almost instantaneous, although some local soreness may remain for a few days, due to soft tissue damage. However, if there is much spasm it is impossible to mobilise the joint. If this is the case, the patient should be put in a collar to immobilise and support the neck, and sent home to rest. Analgesics, muscle relaxants and NSAIDs are also helpful in relieving pain and breaking the pain/spasm vicious cycle. After 1–2 days, the spasm has usually decreased sufficiently to allow manipulation. Following this, the NSAIDs should be continued for 7–10 days, and wearing a soft collar at night holds the neck in a neutral position during sleep. Gentle mobilising exercises should be continued. Sometimes one or two further sessions of manipulation are necessary. Recovery is usually rapid, but the damaged capsule may remain weak, and further stress or an awkward movement may cause a recurrence.

Prolapsed cervical disc

A cervical disc may be damaged acutely by an awkward movement, or more commonly an already worn and damaged disc with a lax annulus fibrosus may have the nucleus pulposus further displaced by a sporting injury, precipitating pain and stiffness in the neck, or nerve root symptoms, or both. Sometimes the symptoms of nerve root irritation predominate. Pain, paraesthesiae and weakness may be noted in the upper limb, or shoulder, or in the case of upper cervical spine lesions, there may be pain in the occipital region. The pain varies from a dull ache to a very severe pain. There may be no pain in the neck itself, but there is usually some limitation of movement on formal testing. Spasm may be very severe, and virtually block all cervical movement. The tendon reflexes may be depressed or absent — biceps jerk is root C5, supinator C6 and triceps C7. There may be motor weakness in the muscles supplied by the affected root. Decreased sensation to pinprick may be elicited within the distribution of the relevant dermatome.

The X-rays may be normal, though there is usually some loss of lordosis due to muscle spasm. Where there has been previous wear and tear or trauma, there may be narrowing of one or more disc spaces, often with osteophyte formation visible anteriorly where the lax annulus fibrosus has pulled on the vertebral periosteum. If the level of the X-ray changes correlate with that of the neurological signs and pain distribution, it is reasonable to assume further bulging or extrusion of disc contents at this level has precipitated the current attack of symptoms.

A collar will keep the neck still and usually relieves pain and spasm, although occasionally people find it intolerable. A soft foam collar can be worn at night, and a firmer Evasote or Plasterozote collar during the daytime. These are usually adequate, but if necessary a rigid polypropylene collar can be used. Analgesics and muscle relaxants help break the pain/spasm cycle, and NSAIDs should be started, as they reduce local tissue swelling. Manipulation may reduce the prolapse and relieve pain, spasm and root irritation, and it is worth a try, provided it is done by someone properly trained and skilled in these techniques.

Whiplash injury

Sudden deceleration or other movements causing excessive flexion/extension of the neck may partially tear the paraspinal ligaments. Typically the victim feels surprisingly well immediately after the incident, but over the next 12–24 hours, the neck becomes progressively stiffer and more painful as an acute inflammatory reaction develops in the damaged tissues. On examination there is tight spasm and movement is limited or absent. The neck is very painful and there may be generalised tenderness. There are no neurological signs. X-ray is normal.

Manipulation and traction are of no help in these cases. The neck should be rested by wearing a collar — a firm Evasote or Plasterzote collar during the daytime, and a softer foam collar at night. If it is very painful, bed rest for the first few days is recommended. Analgesics, muscle relaxants and NSAIDs should be used.

Recovery is usually slow. As the pain and spasm subside the collar can be removed for short periods, and gentle mobilising exercises performed. Gradually the collar can be left off for longer periods, but the pace of recovery should not be forced.

HEAD INJURIES AND CONCUSSION

Any person who is knocked unconscious should be taken to hospital for assessment and observation so there can be prompt surgical intervention if there are signs of intracranial bleeding. This is a generally accepted course of action.

The difficulties of management arise with players who are knocked out for a few seconds only, or who retain consciousness but suffer some confusion and retrograde amnesia. They are suffering from concussion, which is due to rotational, or acceleration-deceleration forces causing the brain within its meninges to lurch violently inside the cranium, and bang against the bones of the skull (see Fig. 16.5). There is an alteration in electrical activity and microscopic structural damage. Repeated injuries of this type cause further damage, until there is demonstrable neurological deficit — the punch-drunk syndrome.

All players suffering loss of consciousness, however brief, or a period of confusion, should be removed from play. They may complain of blurred vision, dizziness, nausea, vomiting and head-ache. On questioning, it may become apparent that they are confused and suffering some retrograde amnesia. There is a danger that this syndrome may be associated with cerebral contusion and intacranial bleeding. The patient should therefore be examined carefully for changes in pupil size or alterations in limb mobility. Bed rest for 24

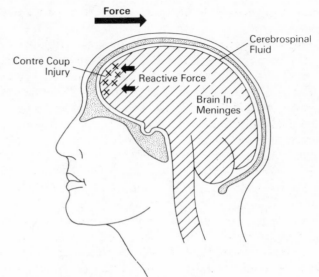

Fig. 16.5. Mechanism underlying concussion.

hours is then advisable, with continued careful observation for changes in mental or physical state. On no account should the patient be left to 'sleep it off' unobserved.

There is a troublesome post-concussion syndrome characterised by recurrent headaches, nausea, dizziness and poor concentration, which may last for 6–8 weeks. Provided there are no abnormal physical signs, the prognosis is excellent. The fundi should be examined to make sure there is no papilloedema. It is said that this syndrome is less trouble if the patient has 24 hours bed rest after the accident.

Return to contact sports should be delayed to avoid a recurrence of symptoms, or a further accident due to impaired concentration or co-ordination. This lay-off should be 1 month after an episode of brief unconsciousness, or at least 2 months if the patient has been unconscious for longer than a few minutes.

Further Reading

Anderson J.R. (ed) 1985 *Muir's Textbook of Pathology*, 12th Edn. London: Arnold.

Forster A. and Palastanga N. 1985 *Clayton's Electrotherapy, Theory and Practice*, 9th Edn. Eastbourne: Baillière Tindall.

Evans P.J. 1986 *The Knee Joint*. London: Churchill Livingstone.

Helal B., King J.B. and Grange W.J. (eds) 1986 *Sports Injuries and their Treatment*. London: Chapman and Hall.

Sperryn P.N. 1983 *Sports and Medicine*. Sevenoaks: Butterworths.

Taussig M.J. 1984 *Processes in Pathology and Microbiology*, 2nd Edn. Oxford: Blackwell Scientific Publications.

Williams J.G.P. 1980 *A Colour Atlas of Injury in Sport*. London: Wolfe Medical.

Williams P.L. and Warwick R. (eds) 1980 *Gray's Anatomy*, 36th Edn. Edinburgh: Churchill Livingstone.

Index